DAVID
SINNER AND BELIEVER

Carlo-Maria Martini

DAVID
SINNER AND BELIEVER

 St Paul Publications

Original title: *Davide peccatore e credente*. © Edizioni Piemme S.p.A. 1989
& Centro Ambrosiano Documentazione e Studi Religiosi 1989

Translated from the Italian by Alan Neame

St Paul Publications
Middlegreen, Slough SL3 6BT, England

English translation copyright © St Paul Publications 1990

ISBN 085439 322 6

Typeset by Grove Graphics, Tring
Printed by Dotesios Printers Ltd., Trowbridge, Wiltshire

St Paul Publications is an activity of the priests and brothers of the
Society of St Paul who proclaim the Gospel through the media of social
communication

Contents

Foreword

The present volume, *David sinner and believer*, contains the meditations and homilies that together made up a course of Spiritual Exercises preached in July 1988 by Cardinal Carlo-Maria Martini, Archbishop of Milan, to the Jesuit Fathers and other missionaries of both sexes, called to conduct their apostolate in Chad.

The Spiritual Exercises are, for those who do them, an episode in salvation history. There is therefore a close relationship between the Exercises and the Bible.

Adopting Ignatius Loyola's method set out in the saint's celebrated little book *Spiritual Exercises*, the Archbishop reflects on the figure of David, the Old Testament king of the Chosen People, with the aim of deepening our awareness of God's saving plan which ultimately shines forth in Christ Jesus.

Since the whole purpose of our Christian life is for us to become aware of being children of God in Jesus, hence a progressive advance towards identification with Christ, the only begotten Son of the Father, it is of very great importance to grasp how the Old Testament represents the way towards this goal.

Jesus is proclaimed as being the fulfilment of the ancient Scriptures; he brings to perfection and concludes the design that begins with Abraham and runs through the Davidic messianic kingly office.

If we leave the Old Testament out of account, we are always in danger of deviating into a view of either a Jesus as revolutionary and political liberator or a Jesus outside history altogether, thus preventing contemplation of the true Jesus Christ, Lord of our life and the entire human environment.

So, to understand Jesus and his gospel, we must know what the preparatory stages were, foreordained by God in the Old Testament.

In this connexion, the titles of the Cardinal's meditations are of particular significance. As they appear in the table of Contents, they mark the successive stages by which the exercitants come to appreciate the figure of David and the other great witnesses of the Hebrew people. David is the type of the man after God's own heart, and he isn't this for any superior morality on his part but because of his faith, his obedience to the Lord, his sense of God's transcendent holiness. The comparison between the temporal king, David, and the universal king, Jesus, is stimulating and rich in instruction: a comparison the Archbishop carries to the very roots in his attempt to find in the story of David some document akin to the New Testament infancy gospels. This he does at the end of the Exercises in his reflections on Ruth, the ancestress of David and hence of Jesus too.

There is no need to emphasise the value of the Spiritual Exercises for Christian life. Even so, it is worth reminding the reader how original St Ignatius Loyola's book is. In a television interview given on July 1, 1988, Cardinal Martini remarked that the book "was written to teach one how to think like a Christian" and he defined it as "a most interesting mental journey, since it leads us to discover how certain things attract us and then delude us, while others that initially alarm us end by taking over our lives".

The Church, for its part, has always encouraged the practice of the Spiritual Exercises. Pius XI, in the encyclical *Mens nostra* of 1929, made a point of stating that "of all methods of spiritual exercises . . . that of the Exercises of St Ignatius is most to be recommended and the most fruitful".

The style of the Archbishop's meditations is very informal and straightforward, without digressions into problems of criticism, which makes *David sinner and believer* all the more enthralling. The individual reader is invited to follow in the footsteps of the original exercitants and thus be led to the discovery of things old and new in the treasure of salvation. Certain it is, this book will help every Christian to see him or herself more clearly in relation to the Jewish people and admit to being still a long way away from full assimilation of the person and message of Christ, even though already grafted into him by baptism.

Introduction

1) Let us begin by reading *Psalm 63* which I have chosen as the key-note of these Exercises. Its Hebrew title is:

A Psalm of David, when he was in the Wilderness of Judah

O GOD, thou art my God, I seek thee,
　my soul thirsts for thee;
my flesh faints for thee,
　as in a dry and weary land where no water is.
So I have looked upon thee in the sanctuary,
　beholding thy power and glory.
Because thy steadfast love is better than life,
　my lips will praise thee.
So I will bless thee as long as I live;
　I will lift up my hands and call on thy name.

My soul is feasted as with marrow and fat,
　and my mouth praises thee with joyful lips,
when I think of thee upon my bed,
　and meditate on thee in the watches of the night;
for thou hast been my help,
　and in the shadow of thy wings I sing for joy.
My soul clings to thee;
　thy right hand upholds me.

But those who seek to destroy my life
　shall go down into the depths of the earth;
they shall be given over to the power of the sword,
　they shall be prey for jackals.
But the king shall rejoice in God;
　all who swear by him shall glory;
　for the mouths of liars will be stopped.

As you know, the Hebrew titles of the Psalms are not original, although they are very ancient. I must however emphasise that they were embedded in Israelite memory and that Jesus read Psalm 63 as the song, the cry in which David expressed his most ardent yearning for God.

2) I have chosen it because, during the days of this Retreat, I intend to reflect on the figure of David.

— He indeed, after Jesus, is the first person to be named in the New Testament: "The genealogy of Jesus Christ, the son of David" (*Mt 1:1*), and in the New Testament his name recurs fifty-nine times.

In the Old, moreover, the longest historical narratives are devoted to him: a large part of the *First Book of Samuel* and all the *Second Book*; the beginning of the *First Book of Kings*; several passages in the *Chronicles*. The prophets Isaiah, Jeremiah, Ezechiel, Amos and Zechariah quote him, as also does the *Book of Wisdom*. Seventy-three *Psalms* are attributed to him in their titles.

With Abraham and Moses, David is one of the three great figures in the Old Testament. As in previous years I have given courses of Exercises on Abraham and Moses respectively, I thought I should take advantage of the present opportunity to reflect more deeply on David. Not merely for the pleasure or interest in studying this great figure of course, but to come to a better understanding of Jesus Christ. In Mark's gospel, the words of the blind man of Jericho's stupendous prayer are: "Jesus, Son of David, have mercy on me!" (*Mk 10:47–48*).

At the beginning of the *Letter to the Romans*, Paul writes of having been called to proclaim "the gospel of God which he promised beforehand through his prophets in the Holy Scriptures, the gospel concerning his Son, who was descended from David according to the flesh" (*Rom 1:1–3*). And in the *Acts of the Apostles* we read that God, having deprived Saul of the kingdom, "raised up David to be their king, of whom he testified: I have found in David the son of Jesse *a man after my heart*, who will do all my will" (*Acts 13:22*).

To know David means to know Jesus better. If however we don't succeed in absorbing the Old Testament message, we shall know Jesus out of historical context and to some degree invent him for ourselves, making him a sociological, humanistic or futuristic figure.

Jesus is the Son of David, in whom the promise made to David is fulfilled; he is the Son of God who becomes man by passing through David's race and the history of his people. For this reason it is most important to give deep thought to those texts that speak of David.

Hence the grace we should ask of the Lord, so to be able to meditate on David as to reach that sublime knowledge of Jesus spoken of by St Paul (cf *Philemon 3:8*).

— And I have other reasons too for reflecting on David. Bishop Ambrose, my predecessor in the See of Milan, devoted two works of exegesis to him: *De interpellatione Job et David* and *De apologia prophetae David*, and dealt at length with him in his sermons to the Milanese. A number of scholars are therefore inclined to date the *Apologia* to the year 388 — one thousand six hundred years ago — when his growing problems with the Emperor Theodosius prompted him to meditate extensively on the ancient king, comparing himself to the prophet Nathan and the Emperor to David, in the hope of inducing Theodosius to repent.

Furthermore, knowing about David is extremely useful for us in understanding the basic meditation proposed by Ignatius Loyola in his book of the *Spiritual Exercises*, when he says: "The first point is to place before my eyes a human king chosen by our Lord God himself" (*n. 92*). According to Scripture, David is that human king designated by the Lord, he is the archetype of the king chosen by God and this is why he is helpful to us in contemplating the eternal king, Jesus.

Our Retreat has no other purpose than a deeper contemplation of Jesus our king.

3) I shall therefore suggest a certain type of biblical reading for you, choosing those episodes from the *First* and *Second Books of Samuel* which best correspond to the thrust of the Exercises as tending to a deeper search for the will of God in Jesus. Not accidentally have I chosen *Psalm 63* as the keynote of our meditations, since in it we find

that basic disposition: *the yearning for God*. "O God, thou art my God, I seek thee" are perhaps the loveliest, most exalted words ever attributed to David.

At this the beginning of our Retreat, we are summoned to reawaken within us that yearning, Lord, for you, of which David was one of the greatest singers.

— "I seek thee", in the ancient versions, is written: "I get up at dawn to be near thee", my first desire, when I wake up, art thou. It is characteristic of our psychology that when we wake up, the first thing we think about is either that which we much desire or much fear.

— "My soul thirsts for thee". This yearning is likened to thirst in the desert where, no water being there, human beings yearn for it with their whole physical nature.

— "My flesh faints for thee"; without thee, I am bereft of nourishment, I have no strength.

These words describe the human being, any one of us. Perhaps our many daily activities prevent us from grasping this clearly, but in fact we have an unassuageable thirst for God and we must give this every encouragement.

Let us say together:

'My God, I pray you to awaken in me that desire for you which is within me and is truly the greatest desire of my life. Sometimes I may forget this; even so I know it to be the unique driving-force of my existence. Whatever I achieve, whatever I think, whatever I express, wells up from the depths of my desire for you. For myself and all those who are to do these Exercises, I ask you to make us aware of our need for you, to let it gush forth like living water, so that we may live with you as David did, who sang to you in the solitude of the wilderness of Judah. Grant that the cry wrung from his heart may become our cry, so that we may rediscover whatever is truest within us as human beings.'

May the Virgin Mary who yearned to see the day of the Messiah, who yearned to see the face of God, help us and be with us, so that this same yearning may burst from our hearts and be nourished by the Word.

1
God loves David

For the prayer that begins this meditation I have taken my inspiration from the first verse of *Psalm 63*: "O God, thou art my God, I seek thee".

'Grant me, O God, to seek you as God. Inspire my heart with the words with which you inspired the Apostle Thomas when at the sight of your resurrected Son he exclaimed: My Lord and my God. Put the word my *into my heart, to indicate that he is my all in all in life. O Jesus who on the cross cried out: God, my God, why hast thou forsaken me?, grant me ever to seek you, even when I feel forsaken. Grant us to seek you day by day, dawn by dawn. Make our search be persevering, never wearied, never tired or bored. Father, pour your Holy Spirit into us so that he may make us seek your face. We ask this of you for the sake of your Son our Lord, whose face we are now seeking. We ask this of you through the intercession of the Mother of Jesus, the Virgin Mary, who understood the difference between the Messiah of all nations and the Messiah of one nation. Grant us to understand what Christ is for the human race, by reflecting on the figure of David, your servant, forefather of your Son. Amen.'*

First of all, I should like by way of instruction to remind you of the four components of the Spiritual Exercises, before setting out the meditation for you, entitled: *God loves David*.

The components of the Spiritual Exercises

1) The first is *liturgical prayer*, of which St Ignatius speaks in note n. 20 of the *Exercises*: even if one is living

1

in some isolated place, it is important to be able to attend daily Mass and Vespers.

Here we have Mass, Lauds and Vespers but the important thing is that our liturgical prayer should be performed well, slowly and peacefully, since an extraordinary strength resides in this.

2) *Private prayer*. St Ignatius requires five periods of private prayer. We shall omit the fifth, which is the midnight meditation. Each of us therefore should fix four times in the course of the day, devoting three to reading or listening to the Word in prayer, and one to simple affective prayer. This fourth exercise is performed by leaving even the Bible aside and fixing our gaze on Jesus; it is essential for summing up all the day's feelings in one contemplative outpouring.

3) *Setting out the points* for the meditation. I shall probably give an extended reading from Scripture in the morning and, in the afternoon, if I haven't thought fit to go on with it, I shall give a short instruction. These are two periods involving the preacher of the Retreat. A third is the homily during our Eucharistic celebration.

4) *Communicating in faith*. Faith deteriorates if kept isolated in the heart. We have one form of communicating: in common prayer. For those who feel inclined, however, we shall foregather every evening to share what each of us has been meditating on and thinks may be of value to the others. A very simple, free exchange.

Private communication of faith can also take place between two or three exercitants and, of course, with me. I shall be gladly available.

The first principle and foundation of the story of David

Having defined the purpose of the Spiritual Exercises in the title (cf *n. 21*), St Ignatius at *n. 23* sets out the *First Principle and Foundation*, that is to say, certain truths from which our lives derive and on which we may depend.

For this reason, we should ask ourselves: what is the *first principle* and the *foundation* of David's story? What is the internal dynamic of his story, the basic secret that will explain it all?

While I urge you to read the relevant passages in the *First and Second Book of Samuel* to find the answer to this question for yourselves, in the present meditation I am going to suggest to you what I consider to be the first principle and foundation, hence the key, for our contemplating Jesus through the figure of David.

Then I shall try and apply it to the personal story of each of us here.

— We can assume the opening words of *Psalm 63* as essential to a definition of the life of David. We have already said the Psalter contains seventy-three psalms attributed to him. Even if such attribution is not historically correct, we should certainly take account of the note in the *Jerusalem Bible*: "It is reasonable to hold that there must be some connection between the Davidic collection and David himself. Taking into account what the historical books have to say of his musical talent (*1 Sam 16:16–18*; cf *Amos 6:5*), his poetic gifts (*2 Sam 1:19–27; 3:33–34*), and his love of the liturgy (*2 Sam 6:5,15–16*), it would seem inevitable that these qualities should be expressed in the Psalter . . . and David, who 'sang the songs of Israel' (*2 Sam 23:1*), must be conceded an essential part in the formation of the religious poetry of the Chosen People" (cf *Introduction to the Psalms*).

Hence we should adopt the point of view of the Jewish people, of Jesus who prayed the psalms, attributing them to David.

Not for nothing have I already said that *Psalm 63* is of great interest: it shows how the entire story of David is sustained by his search, his burning desire for God. Weak and sinful, he cleaves strongly to God nonetheless and yearns for him above all things. He loves the people of his village, he loves his friends, he loves women, he loves war, but he loves God more than all the rest.

Psalm 18 too, with its title *"To the choirmaster. A psalm of David the servant of the Lord, who addressed the words of this song to the Lord on the day when the Lord delivered him from the hand of all his enemies and from the hand of Saul"*, expresses this burning love: "I love thee, O Lord, my strength". This is his life's grand refrain, his secret.

— Yet it seems to me that this may be only apparently so. If, for instance, we read *Psalm 18* not in the Psalter — which represents a more recent recension of the text — but rather in the *Second Book of Samuel (22:2f)*, which has the title *Psalm of David*, we shall get a surprise. Instead of "I love thee, O Lord, my strength", we find: "The Lord is my rock and my fortress and my deliverer, my God".

Here I see the first principle and deeper foundation of David's life: not that he loves God and yearns for him, but that *God loves David*.

The *Song of Solomon* speaks of a youth who, in Hebrew, is always called "Dod" or "Dodi", that is to say, "Beloved", "my Beloved". The Hebrew letters are the same as those of the name "David", who is thus the beloved, God's beloved, he whom God loves.

The epithet used for John the evangelist springs to mind: "the one whom Jesus loved" (*Jn 13:23*).

The key to David's life is that God loves him and, in this context, we shall reflect on the three accounts of the way David was chosen.

Textual critics argue over whether there are three separate traditions but in the spirit of interpreting the Bible as a whole we can make the most of what the text has to offer by affirming that there are in fact three ways in which God loves David and calls him to him.

The three vocation narratives occur in *1 Samuel 16 & 17* and I invite you to read them very carefully during our time here.

Before we look at them together, I should like to draw your attention to a passage in *2 Samuel 7*, that great chapter written expressly to draw the whole story of David into a unity. It was probably a later addition and is the chapter most often quoted in the Psalms, in the Prophets and in the New Testament: the annunciation to Mary, the seventeenth chapter of St John's gospel and the Acts of the Apostles all echo this chapter.

Verses 8–9 are the ones that interest us. King David wants to build a temple and the prophet Nathan approves. During the night however the word of the Lord is revealed to Nathan, who passes it on to David in obedience to God's command: "Now therefore thus you shall say to my servant David, 'Thus says the Lord of hosts, I took you from the pasture, from following the sheep, that you should be prince over my people Israel; and I have been with you wherever you went, and have cut off all your enemies from before you; and I will make for you a great name, like the name of the great ones of the earth' " (*2 Sam 7:8–9*).

The whole of David's story is summed up in this loving initiative of God's, which in the passage quoted is put on record by the Lord himself: from unknown shepherd to important personage.

Now we are in a position to consider the three calls:
— the first call is by divine election;
— the second call is circumstantial;
— the third is the call that entails the chosen one's taking a risk.

There are, you might say, three ways through which God expresses his love.

1) *1 Samuel 16:1–13*. The account is extremely well known. Samuel has been ordered to go and offer a sacrifice and, among the sons of Jesse, to seek the king whom the Lord has chosen. The description, of a very high literary order, shows Samuel having the sons of Jesse pass before him one by one. But the Lord keeps warning the prophet that the right one hasn't yet appeared. Eventually they send for the youngest, who is out pasturing the flocks. When he arrives in front of Samuel, the Lord says: "Stand up and anoint him; he's the one" (cf *v. 12*).

There is no particular merit in the lad, no predisposition whatever. Indeed, what might pass for suitability humanly speaking, gets rejected, as we read in *v. 6* with regard to Eliab: "Do not look on his appearance or on the height of his stature, because I have rejected him". Eliab, the eldest, was tall, very strong and presumptuous with it. Indeed, when in chapter 17 David is prepared to take the risk

involved in accepting Goliath's challenge, Eliab actually
rebukes him: "Now Eliab his eldest brother heard when he
spoke to the men; and Eliab's anger was kindled against
David, and he said, 'Why have you come down? And with
whom have you left those few sheep in the wilderness? I
know your presumption, and the evil of your heart; for you
have come down to see the battle' " (*v. 28*), while I'm here
doing my duty in the service of my country.

We understand quite easily why the Lord rejects Eliab.
But he then rejects all the other brothers, until the youngest
one appears, who "was ruddy and had beautiful eyes, and
was comely" (cf *v. 12*). The description underlines the fact
that he isn't suited to be king. Saul was chosen because
"from his shoulders upward he was taller" than any man
in Israel (cf *1 Sam 9:2*). The king in those days was first
and foremost the leader in war. Hence David, ruddy and
of comely aspect, cannot become a warrior and lead into
battle; he cannot be set at the head of his people, he is not
fiery-eyed, not born to command.

He is a good friend, a simple soul, but he is loved by the
Lord: "Samuel took the horn of oil and anointed him in
the midst of his brothers; and the Spirit of the Lord came
mightily upon David from that day forward" (*v. 13*). There
is an assonance here with the *Letter to the Romans*: "God's
love has been poured into our hearts through the Holy Spirit
which has been given to us" (*Rom 5:5*).

The first component of the call is the pure benevolence
of God.

In point of fact, this account is never referred to again
in what follows. It remains God's secret, his own plan
investing David with the Spirit.

2) *1 Samuel 16:14–23*. The second call, in a certain sense,
ignores the previous one and is the expression of circumstances obtaining at the time.

Saul is a disturbed personality and subject to attacks of
melancholia. At this point in time he is particularly
depressed because he knows he has been rejected by the
Lord, and he is miserable because Samuel has deserted him.
So he wants someone to play the lyre to him. Somebody

knows of David and his musical talents; word gets about and reaches Saul, who has David summoned to court: "Saul sent messengers to Jesse and said, 'Send me David your son (who is with the sheep)'. And Jesse took an ass laden with bread, and a skin of wine and a kid, and sent them by David his son to Saul. And David came to Saul and entered his service" (*vv. 19–20*). From this moment, David's career begins.

The circumstances were fortuitous, unforeseen, since Saul's choice might well not have fallen on him; evidently God was at work by means of chance.

3) *1 Samuel 17:12–39*. The third mode of calling entails courage, the taking of a personal risk, and this accords well enough with the previous two, that is, of accepting the divine choice and of seeing God's guiding intervention in circumstances.

The first part of the chapter is the terrifying description of Goliath, which reminds us of St Ignatius's description of the Enemy, in the meditation on Two Standards (cf *Second Week n. 140*).

Then comes David's chance arrival; he has come bringing cheese, grain and bread for his brothers who are in camp. He hears people talking about Goliath, he listens to the Philistine's threats against God and asks how on earth it can be they allow him to insult the Israelites and why no one takes up the challenge. Eliab — whom we have seen already — tells him to mind his own business; David is astounded at his brother's reaction. So he puts the same question to someone else. At this point, "when the words which David spoke were heard, they repeated them before Saul; and he sent for him. And David said to Saul, 'Let no man's heart fail because of him; your servant will go and fight with this Philistine.' And Saul said to David, 'You are not able to go against this Philistine to fight with him; for you are but a youth, and he has been a man of war from his youth.' But David said to Saul, 'Your servant used to keep sheep for his father; and when there came a lion, or a bear, and took a lamb from the flock, I went after him and smote him and delivered it out of his mouth; and if he arose against me, I caught him by his beard' " (*vv. 31–35*).

Thus David takes his risk, in the name of the Lord. His words deserve lengthy meditation on our part. Although he counts on the fact that God has always protected him, he nonetheless performs an act of courage which puts his own life at stake. The risk he takes is a real one since it is a matter of victory or death; it isn't a test or an experiment.

This is the moment when David fully accepts his call.

The first principle and foundation of my own life

Let us now reflect on the first principle and foundation of our own personal story.

1) Divine election: God has chosen me, and he has loved me. This is all, this is the fundamental truth of my life; it defines me as a human being. If he hadn't loved me first, I should not be here today. Something might happen to me, I might lose my vocation, grace, even faith, but it still remains true that God loves me and that on this first principle and foundation I can always build everything anew.

In matchless words Paul sings of God's immeasurable, free initiative: "He chose us in him before the foundation of the world . . . In him we have redemption . . . He has made known to us the mystery of his will . . . to unite all things under one sole Head, the Christ . . . In him we have been made heirs, destined by his design . . . to the praise of his glory (cf *Eph 1:3–14*).

The verse of *Psalm 63*: "O God, thou art my God, I seek thee", becomes clearer. God never wishes to lose the initiative of salvation, of mercy, of tenderness, directed towards me; and he constantly arouses in me the desire to seek him.

2) Reflecting on our own lives, we perceive that for us too there has been the interplay of many circumstances. In this connection I recall the reply I got from Hans-Urs von Balthasar which reached me a day or two after his

death; he was acknowledging a note of mine to congratulate him on having been nominated a Cardinal: "He was pleased to honour me, but he could have chosen somebody else".

Consider for instance all those companions and friends of ours, better men and women than we are, who have not been called to the priestly or religious vocation. Consider the ones who, having been called, have given up, owing to the extremely harsh, maybe intolerable circumstances in which they found themselves.

In our own lives, by way of contrast, everything has worked to one end, in our favour. But God it is who has loved us in these diverse situations and allowed us to recognise his activity. I myself, if I enjoy the privilege of being here to pray with you, owe this to my being a bishop — a matter of the purest chance.

God's love is present in every detail of our existence and his design gradually becomes easier to see. Events seem fortuitous, disconnected, as for David, and yet God works to the very hour of our death, putting into effect his secret project of mercy.

Because of this, we ought to have an immense trust in life, come what may; and we shall also need discernment, to pay attention to the circumstances by means of which we are being guided.

Some of you have spoken to me about the vicissitudes of war and famine and how these have produced a new spiritual impetus. Terrible moments which could have been regarded as capricious tricks of fate, have instead been interpreted as the effect of God's love in action. There are two ways of looking at situations and of understanding our existence.

3) Finally, our life is based on having the courage to take an absolute risk. Once we stop taking risks for the Kingdom, we are finished, psychologically speaking, we're old.

And the risk demands freedom of spirit, inner joy, youthful daring.

Today, in the Western world at least, young people don't

have this sort of courage. They seek experiences — in love, in friendship — but are scared of making the definitive choice.

This seems to me to be one of the curses of our century, for being human is itself a risk, and vocation demands that risks be taken. When we forget that God's love is leading us, we see events as the product of the evil genius, Power, crushing us, and so we take defensive measures, we weigh the odds, we grow timid and incapable of taking a chance.

The figure of David shows us the courage to be a bit mad, not to pause overlong to assess our resources, our health, other people's reactions.

'Lord, we thank you for giving us the courage to accept the risk inherent in our mission in this part of Africa, and we ask you to give us joy ever new with which to praise your love for us.'

For your private prayer I suggest you quietly read over the scriptural passages and then consider your own story up to today.

I am certain the Virgin Mary will help us to realise how important it is for us to accept the divine initiative, our circumstances and the risk we have to face day by day; for living means letting things take their course where those who are called, as we have been, are concerned. Prayer itself is a risk when we are not aware of an encounter. Believing, self-surrender: this is the secret of earthly life that Jesus, Son of David, has taught us.

THE HUMBLE ECONOMY OF THE KINGDOM
(Homily for Monday in the XVI week "per annum")

The readings for today's liturgy are taken from chapters 12 and 13 of the gospel according to Matthew.

Having proclaimed and preached the Kingdom, Jesus begins to speak, from chapter 11 onwards, about the mystery of the Kingdom and about its humble economy, so that it may be either accepted or rejected.

The most significant passage perhaps is in the prayer: "I thank thee, Father, Lord of heaven and earth, that thou hast hidden these things from the wise and understanding and revealed them to babes" (*11:25*). This is the key to the organisation of the subsequent discourses: the great and the wise don't understand the humble economy of the Kingdom, while babes do.

Today's text (*12:38–42*) deals with the rejection of those who do not believe in Jesus, and we can divide it into three points:

First, the request for signs: "Teacher, we wish to see a sign from you" (*v. 38*).

Next, Jesus's general condemnation: "An evil and adulterous generation seeks for a sign!" (*v. 39a*).

Lastly, the counter-sign given by the Master: "No sign shall be given to it except the sign of the prophet Jonah" (*v. 39b*).

1) What does asking the Lord for a sign actually mean?

Note: the scribes and Pharisees express a desire, and we have already said that desire for God is the motor-power of the entire story of David. Here however we have a debasement of the religious demand, since here there is no faith in the Lord to support it.

If we seek a divine sign because we are truly seeking God, why, then, we have the sacraments, prayer, the very life of the Church? All these are signs, revealing God in one aspect, concealing him in another.

When however we merely seek a sign, as the scribes and Pharisees were doing, then the quest is no longer genuinely religious. Gradually the yearning for God is forgotten and the sign as such is what is desired.

And so we fall into the economy of success and reject the humble economy of the Kingdom. Of course, we don't admit this; we insist that we're seeking success for God's sake, to give glory to his Name, to honour him. In fact, however, we come to a halt, confined within a sign that gratifies and comforts us instead.

2)   But Jesus doesn't consent to this, hence his fierce reaction to their request: "*Adulterous* generation!" Instead of seeking God, you want a substitute, a different love, a love of this world. It isn't wicked in itself to seek signs, at times when only through these can we reach our God; what is wicked is to linger over the signs, according them an importance they do not have.

Perverse generation, in the sense that *it isn't straightforward*, doesn't act right, doesn't have its gaze fixed on God, no longer dares take a risk but prefers to be guided by signs reinforcing it in its convictions, eliminating all risk.

Such a desire is more common than one might think. Often, in the exercise of my mystery, I find myself asking for signs: Suggest an effective way to prevent the young from deserting the parish church!

In fact there are no ways of guaranteeing pastoral success. And it is absolutely useless to keep foraging through the books or pursuing the latest creations of the pastoral imagination, in the hope that eventually those who have drifted away will return to the Church, and that everything then will check out neatly! On the contrary, what is needed is to take a chance in the dark.

For this reason I am apprehensive about the spread, in Europe at any rate, of apparitions of the Virgin. Possibly it is a sign of Our Lady's love, of her desire to encourage us; but when the crowds assemble to receive oracular sayings, to obtain reassurance of being on the right path, and not to accept the risk of faith and of the difficult choice in life, we ought to be seriously alarmed. These apparitions cannot monopolise the centre of Christian life; and if they do, this means that for a part of the faithful, the quest has taken the wrong direction.

Jesus teaches that economy of faith which is prepared to accept lack of success, even failure, of a project. He denounces that request for signs, the ultimate effect of which is to negate the true search for God alone. The false worship of signs, even ecclesiastical ones, is an ever present idolatry in our hearts, by which we seek to obtain at all cost what we want, whereas what God wants above all is trust, surrender to him, absolute faith.

3) *"No sign shall be given to it except the sign of the prophet Jonah."* It is hard to be sure how to interpret this passage when we consider the various nuances proposed by our exegetes.

Jesus refused to give a sign, nor for that matter can he give a sign so radical. In Luke's gospel (cf *11:29–32*) it seems it might be the preaching as such: I am the sign, talking to you now, telling you to follow me, to shut your eyes and jump.

In Matthew this may be so too, yet the emphasis is on the sign of the prophet Jonah who was known and honoured for having spent three days inside a fish. "As Jonah was three days and three nights in the belly of the whale, so will the Son of man be three days and three nights in the heart of the earth". Certainly these words are full of mystery to the listener. Sometimes it is said Jesus is alluding to his own resurrection; I myself take the view that in fact he is alluding to his death.

Christ's death is the sign. Nothing whatever is said about his rising again after three days. The sign is the cross, the sojourn in the abyss of death, defeat, hidden existence.

In this sense it is a counter-sign. To those who seek startling signs, Jesus announces his own death, his own departure into gloom and darkness.

Of course the Resurrection is evoked, implicit as it were in his dying for love, in the faith the Son has in the Father culminating in the cross.

The scandal of the cross is the great sign of a love that, unbelievably, goes to death.

So, if Jesus always talks in parables so as not to frighten us too much, we know the great mystery of God's dying for love invites us to contemplate our own baptismal calling to die with him; to contemplate the economy of the victorious cross in contrast to the economy of success, the clamorous economy of the world.

'O Jesus, you make all this present for us in the Eucharist. You ask us to celebrate the humble, hidden economy of your entry into death for love's sake, to celebrate the gift of the Holy Spirit poured out from the cross and the mystery of the resurrection and of the life that flows from your sacrifice. Teach us, Lord Jesus, to live this Eucharist in attentiveness to your Word, seeking under the sign of bread and wine God who bestows himself in fullness of love and our gift to you, in response to yours, in the grace of the Holy Spirit and through the intercession of the Virgin Mary your Mother.'

2

Purposes of the Exercises

For the prayer to introduce this instruction, I have drawn my inspiration from *Psalm 18*, also known as the *Royal Te Deum*, where we read: "Yes, thou dost light my lamp; the Lord my God lightens my darkness" (*v. 29*). The same expression is also to be found in the song in the *Second Book of Samuel*: "Yea, thou art my lamp, O Lord, and my God lightens my darkness" (*22:29*).

Probably the older reading is the one in *2 Samuel 22*: "Thou art my lamp, O Lord".

'I pray you, Lord, above all to light my lamp, which is prayer. Prayer which takes an effort to light, which isn't as brilliant as I should wish. I beg you, Lord, to light it so that I can more boldly make those words of David's mine: Thou art *my lamp. Hence I do not intend to worry over-much about my own prayer, not even during the retreat I'm now making, since I am certain that you are my lamp, the sun of my life. Grant, Lord our God, that we, having your light to enlighten us, may grasp the mystery of prayer, the mystery of a spiritual retreat, the mystery of how to cultivate devotion.*

Grant me to cultivate my ground in humility and simplicity of heart, in imitation of the Virgin Mary. We ask you this for the sake of Christ Jesus, your Son and our Lord.'

During this instruction we shall be talking about the purposes of the Exercises, of which there are at least three:
— to seek the will of God,
— to cultivate devotion;
— to re-learn how to pray.

Seeking the will of God

In the classic vision of the *Spiritual Exercises* there is one original, fundamental purpose; *to seek the will of God.*

In this text, st Ignatius writes that the purpose of the entire undertaking is "to seek and find the will of God concerning the ordering of life for the salvation of one's soul" (*Annotation n. 1*).

This purpose keeps recurring in the fundamental meditations, for example in the *Second Week* at *n. 150*, three categories of persons are spoken of who desire to save their souls and to find peace in God. And in *n. 155* he speaks of the third category of persons "who desire nothing except as God shall inspire them to wish". These are other ways of expressing the intention "to seek the will of God".

But how are we to explain, theologically speaking, what is meant by this formula which, where St Ignatius is concerned, means the search for the will of God *shining forth in Jesus Christ*?

Let us begin by saying how the search for the will of God is *not* considered in the Exercises.

David, for instance, seeks the will of God by consulting the Lord: "Shall I go and attack these Philistines?" (*1 Samuel 23:2*). His is a somewhat magical, oracular search, a kind of seeking of signs to have a sure answer. It is as though the will of God were hidden in a certain place and could eventually be found.

In the Exercises, this is not the way to seek the will of God. It was all right for David but, as St John of the Cross writes, under the new law of the gospel there is no further cause to question God, nor for him to speak or answer as in the days of the old law. For in jesus the entire will of God is revealed (cf *Ascent of Mount Carmel, book II, chapter XXIII, 3*).

I therefore suggest some short theological theses which explain what is meant by the will of God shining forth in Jesus Christ.

1) God wishes to communicate himself, he wishes to give himself. "It pleases God in his goodness and wisdom

to reveal himself and to make known the mystery of his will, by means of which the human race, through Jesus Christ, the Word made flesh, in the Holy Spirit has access to the Father and is made a participant in the divine nature'' (*Dei Verbum, 2*).

In this revelation the invisible God in his immense love turns to the human race as though to friends and converses with us, inviting us to share his life.

2) This wish of God's to communicate himself is perfectly fulfilled in Jesus who is the means, the purpose, communication at its fullest, and fruit of the divine will.

Jesus Christ is God's will communicated in manner both absolute and definitive.

3) God's will, so perfectly fulfilled in Christ, is fulfilled, by participation, in the union of Christ with us and mankind at large.

God's plan is Jesus with us, us with Jesus, mankind with Jesus. Hence it is not we who unite ourselves to Jesus but he who draws us to himself.

4) How is the union of mankind with Jesus brought about? By means of the Holy Spirit.

St Thomas Aquinas has a magnificent formula to do with this: ''The law of the New Testament consists principally in the Holy Spirit'', the divine force making one with Christ.

God's will is the Holy Spirit as principle of sanctification and union of mankind with Jesus Christ.

5) What is the union of mankind with Jesus brought about by the Holy Spirit? It is the Church, to be sure; Holy Church welling up from the Spirit in history.

God wills the Church.

6) More precisely, the Holy Spirit wills the local Church, which is the union of certain specific people among themselves and with Christ.

The will of God for me, therefore, is my mode of existence within the Church, and I ought to seek what the Holy Spirit prompts me to do, so that the Church may spread and become complete communication-of-God. And first and foremost the Holy Spirit prompts me to become more and more closely united to Christ Jesus, so that I may be an instrument for uniting others to him.

Everything else — literature, art, economics, be it what it may — is subsidiary to this search for God's will concerning my life in the Church. Normally this occurs once and for all: I mean *vocation*. Hence the Exercises are primarily the method for choosing the right one.

So what then is meant by seeking the will of God in an annual Retreat? Simply to renew our faithfulness to our vocation, seriously to strike out again along the path to perform what the Spirit wants me to be and do in the Church, so that I may become completely one with Jesus and be of help to everyone else.

Through silence, attention to the Word and meditation, let us examine our faithfulness to God's plan for us in everyday events, our faithfulness to achieving union with Christ and with the Church. God wills and asks no more.

Cultivating devotion

An annual Retreat has a second, more specific purpose and I define it in the words of a great spiritual figure, Père Michel Ledrus, formerly professor of spiritual theology at the Gregorian University in Rome. He always used the following formula: "*The annual Exercises are for cultivating devotion*".

In classic speech, devotion means liveliness, freshness, readiness to serve God willingly, from the heart, cheerfully, lovingly, joyfully, courageously. It is thus a most important quality, the loveliest flower of the spiritual life.

Even so, we know people who live their vocation in boredom and gloom, whereas the life led according to the Spirit requires joy and enthusiasm.

Devotion means cheerfully embracing the daily sacrifice, the day's frustrations and those of our apostolic task, aridity in prayer and heart. Devotion thus has to be something God gives us.

We can do our duty, we can obey God, without devotion, without light.

"O God, thou art my lamp": devotion is the divine illumination of our life.

Often we imagine, now having had a variety of experiences, that what counts is to do everything properly, and that's it. True enough: but it isn't actually possible to do things properly, especially when other people are involved, if there's no smile in the soul, no amiability, no cordiality.

Devotion is another aspect of the risk we have already talked about. Taking the risk of confronting tricky situations or awkward people, while saying: Thank you, Lord, since this not as straightforward as it looked! Or: Thank you, I haven't run into problems like these for such a long time!

It seems strange but here lies the strength of the spiritual life. When I am in a good mood and some priest comes along, apologising for telling me about his problems because — he adds — "you have so many of your own", I reply, "Not at all, and thank you very much. The whole point of my being here is to have problems!"

As you see, it isn't easy to give a full explanation of what devotion is. Nevertheless we have to cultivate it, since it does not come of its own but comes from the Lord.

Of their own come hard work, frustration, weariness, nervous strain, exhaustion.

Contrariwise, gifts of God are ease, joy and the ability to simplify.

Perhaps devotion is really the ability to simplify complicated problems.

To cultivate it, to prepare our earthly nature for the gift of devotion, we must spend much time in prayer, in quietly listening to the Word and in prolonged meditation on the Bible.

And it is precisely from prolonged prayer over the Scriptures that the Spirit gushes up like living water for the soul.

Persevering in this type of prayer, unstintingly offering God the appropriate length of time for prayer, being prodigal with it, in the certainty that sooner or later the morning dew of the Holy Spirit will rain down on our aridity:

all this is cultivating devotion and there is nowhere more propitious for this than the annual Retreat.

A practical school of prayer

And so the third purpose of the Retreat is to exercise ourselves in a practical school of prayer, in re-learning to pray.

During our years in the novitiate, we all learned how to pray but since then we have got out of the habit, have lost our taste for it.

There is a very mysterious, very important passage in the *Letter to the Romans*. I have asked prominent exegetes to explain it to me and have invariably received the answer that it was a very difficult thing to do. St Paul writes: "Likewise the Spirit helps us in our weakness; for we do not know how to pray as we ought, but the Spirit himself intercedes for us with sighs too deep for words. And he who searches the hearts of men knows what is in the mind of the Spirit, because the Spirit intercedes for the saints according to the will of God" (*Rom 8:26–28*).

I think the Apostle's words can help us set out again on the way of prayer by suggesting three things to us:

— the prayer we re-learn in the annual Retreat is first and foremost the fruit of humility;

— it is a gift of the Spirit;

— it is joy in the heart.

1) When we have forgotten the practice of prayer, it is reborn in us the moment we admit our own inability. Indeed, St Paul says: "We do not know how to pray as we ought". This is the admission of a mystic who did know how to pray. Perhaps it means we don't know what desires we ought to express to God. In any case, to admit this is a good way of beginning to learn afresh how to pray.

Again: "The Spirit helps us in our weakness". We are weak, just like people without health; we want to pray but we haven't got the strength, the guts to persevere. Into our heads come thoughts about what's got to be done next, of injuries we have sustained in community or outside, resentment that we harbour in our hearts, and we can't find a way of starting to pray. Here we're dealing with a weakness which is part and parcel of human frailty. Not by chance in the Greek text is the term *astheneia* the same as the one used by the Apostle when he says: "While we were *sinners* (*asthenes*), at the right time Christ died for the ungodly" (cf *Rom 5:6*).

The frailty of our heart is to blame; full of complaints, judgements about other people, discontent. When we start praying, this whole burden is likely to reassert itself.

Hence it is essential to realise that deep down in each of us there is an element of impurity, thoughts that are not after God's heart. To confess them is a good start and means re-learning how to pray by making, as St Ignatius suggests, an act of profound adoration: Lord, I am not worthy, I am not capable of praying, I am as nothing before you. Lord, light my lamp, be my lamp, for I cannot organise my prayers myself, since your Holy Spirit alone knows what praying really means.

2) "Likewise the Spirit helps us in our weakness . . . the Spirit himself intercedes for us with sighs too deep for words". These are even more mysterious words.

"Likewise": like what? The reference is to an earlier verse: "The Spirit himself bears witness with our spirit that we are children of God" (*Rom 8:16*). The Spirit that witnesses with us that we are children of God prays for us too with sighs too deep for words.

Exegetes advance various theories to explain the *sighs too deep for words*. The important thing however is that we are talking about a real, deep experience: the Spirit prays within us and intercedes for the saints, and He who searches hearts knows the desire of the Spirit. Desire in the Greek text is *tophronema*, that is to say, the mind of the Spirit, which is that of Christ.

"His intercession for the saints accords with God's designs"; he prays the right way. We cannot know whether our own prayer is right or whether it is turned in on ourselves, whether it is a monologue or a hallucination.

This is why we have to put our trust in the Spirit, in the knowledge of his gift within me. And so, even if we are tired and arid, we can stay before the Blessed Sacrament without forcing ourselves to formulate goodness knows what thoughts, knowing by faith that the Spirit is praying aright within us.

It happens to me, even so, that I feel tired when, during pastoral visits, I have for instance to celebrate a second pontifical Mass on the same day. On these occasions I renew my act of faith, I try to stay calm and perform the liturgical acts correctly, leaving the Holy Spirit to do the rest.

St Paul assures us the Spirit prays within us; this is a truth, not a pious invention, since the Spirit of Jesus, which is the will of God, has been given to us to conform us to the Son who ever "intercedes for us" (*Rom 8:34*). Within us is Jesus praying.

Of course for our part we must persevere long and hard in prayer: gradually we become aware of the presence of the Spirit praying within us.

And I think David, in *Psalm 63*, is indeed expressing the prayer of the Spirit, crying aright to God within him.

3) Prayer is heart's joy; re-learning how to pray means savouring, tasting how sweet the Lord is.

Before coming to Chad I made my annual Retreat with the bishops of the Lombard Region. The director of the retreat was a theologian. Talking to us about prayer, he said that as a boy and later as a seminarian, he had learnt that prayer was a duty; but after years of experience, he had learnt that prayer was joy.

Especially joy in the Psalms, since in these we share David's joy, Jesus's joy, since the Psalms say the very words that we shall want to say before God.

This discovery is bestowed on us with the passing of time; it does not mean that our prayer should be facile or without effort. Joy means depth of spirit, it means savouring God, it means penetrating to the heart of Christ.

Devotion of which we were speaking earlier, is the

experience of this simple yet mysterious joy in God. One little spark of it is worth more than all the good things of this world and, once it has been tasted, one single time, it can never be cancelled from our life.

Conclusion

I invite you to go on meditating on David's three calls and, before the Blessed Sacrament, to contemplate the story of your own life.

As application of the instruction, I suggest you ask yourselves:

— what is the aim I set myself in this Retreat?

— what other purposes do I see besides the three already mentioned?

— what do I understand by cultivating devotion or re-learning to pray?

— will the Lord perhaps grant me to discover a particular purpose he has in mind for me?

May the Virgin Mary help us clearly to find this purpose, whereby we may all be brought closer together.

3

David sinner and believer

*'O God, you are my God, you it was who loved me first,
who love me, you who seek me and desire me. But I too
seek you, my soul thirsts for you, you are my supreme good.*

Who are those, my God, plotting to take my life (cf Ps
63:10), *what is it, driving my soul to its ruin and not allowing me to rejoice in you, not letting me drink at your spring,
preventing me from hearing the cry of my heart?*

*Grant me to understand this, Lord, on this penitential
day, at the school of your servant David, sinner and believer,
sinner but believer'.*

By contemplating David the sinner we shall grasp
something about ourselves and so be able to perform the
first week of St Ignatius's Exercises, that is to say, the
exercises of repentance and confession. In today's meditations we shall reflect on two of David's sins. For David,
though believing in and loving God, was a cruel, vindic-
tive, sensual man. For his cruel treatment of his enemies
suffice it to read *2 Samuel 8:2,4,5*; to his sensuality the
passages *2 Samuel 3:2–5; 5:12f* bear witness; and David's
last words are about revenge (*1 Kings 2:5–6*).

Even so, the Bible presents only two of David's actions
as really and truly sinful, confining itself to telling the rest
without passing judgement. It is worthwhile understanding
why this should be so.

Let us start by reading the more obscure of these accounts
(*2 Samuel 24:1–25*) in that same spirit St Ignatius recommends us to adopt. He says that to seek and find the will
of God we must free ourselves from all inordinate affec-
tions (cf *Annotation n. 1*), in the conviction that there is
always something to hold one back in such a search.

And this conviction is repeated many times over, for

example where he writes: "Spiritual exercises to conquer oneself and regulate one's life, and to avoid coming to a determination through any inordinate affection" (*Title n. 21*)

We have already noted that the royal road for entering into prayer is the recognition of our own frailty and unworthiness.

Let us therefore ask the Holy Spirit to purify our hearts, especially today.

The narrative (2 Samuel 24:1–25)

"Again the anger of the Lord was kindled against Israel, and he incited David against them, saying, "Go, number Israel and Judah." So the king said to Joab and the commanders of the army, who were with him, "Go through all the tribes of Israel, from Dan to Beersheba, and number the people, that I may know the number of the people." But Joab said to the king, "May the Lord your God add to the people a hundred times as many as they are, while the eyes of my lord the king still see it; but why does my lord the king delight in this thing?" But the king's word prevailed against Joab and the commanders of the army. So Joab and the commanders of the army went out from the presence of the king to number the people of Israel. They crossed the Jordan, and began from Aroer, and from the city that is in the middle of the valley, toward Gad and on to Jazer. Then they came to Gilead, and to Kadesh in the land of the Hittites; and they came to Dan, and from Dan they went around to Sidon, and came to the fortress of Tyre and to all the cities of the Hivites and Canaanites; and they went out to the Negeb of Judah at Beersheba. So when they had gone through all the land, they came to Jerusalem at the end of nine months and twenty days. And Joab gave the sum of the numbering of the people to the king: in Israel there were eight hundred thousand valiant men who drew the sword, and the men of Judah were five hundred thousand.

But David's heart smote him after he had numbered the people. And David said to the Lord, "I have sinned greatly in what I have done. But now, O Lord, I pray thee, take away the iniquity of thy servant; for I have done very foolishly.' And when David arose in the morning, the word of the Lord came to the prophet Gad, David's seer, saying, "Go and say to David, 'Thus says the Lord, Three things I offer you; choose one of them, that I may do it to you.' " So Gad came to David and told him, and said to him, "Shall three years of famine come to you in your land? Or will you flee three months before your foes while they pursue you? Or shall there be three days' pestilence in your land? Now consider, and decide what answer I shall return to him who sent me." Then David said to Gad, "I am in great distress; let us fall into the hand of the Lord, for his mercy is great; but let me not fall into the hand of man."

So the Lord sent a pestilence upon Israel from the morning until the appointed time; and there died of the people from Dan to Beersheba seventy thousand men. And when the angel stretched forth his hand toward Jerusalem to destroy it, the Lord repented of the evil, and said to the angel who was working destruction among the people, "It is enough; now stay your hand." And the angel of the Lord was by the threshing floor of Araunah the Jebusite. Then David spoke to the Lord when he saw the angel who was smiting the people, and said, "Lo, I have sinned, and I have done wickedly; but these sheep, what have they done? Let thy hand, I pray thee, be against me and against my father's house."

And Gad came that day to David, and said to him, "Go up, rear an altar to the Lord on the threshing floor of Araunah the Jebusite." So David went up at Gad's word, as the Lord commanded. And when Araunah looked down, he saw the king and his servants coming on toward him; and Araunah went forth, and did obeisance to the king with his face to the ground. And Araunah said, "Why has my lord the king come to his servant?" David said, "To buy the threshing floor of you, in order to build an altar to the Lord, that the plague may be averted from the people." Then Araunah said to David, "Let my lord the

king take and offer up what seems good to him; here are the
oxen for the burnt offering, and the threshing sledges
and the yokes of the oxen for the wood. All this, O king,
Araunah gives to the king.'' And Arau'nah said to the
king, "The Lord your God accept you." But the king
said to Araunah, "No, but I will buy it of you for a price;
I will not offer burnt offerings to the Lord my God
which cost me nothing." So David bought the threshing
floor and the oxen for fifty shekels of silver. And
David built there an altar to the Lord, and offered burnt
offerings and peace offerings. So the Lord heeded
supplications for the land, and the plague was averted from
Israel."

This chapter, probably an addition, is certainly very
strange. The story of David is virtually finished and the
opening pages of the next book, *1 Kings*, deal with David
as an old man, the intrigues over the succession, and then
his death.

Yet, having reported the king's last words in chapter 23,
the Bible now presents us with this narrative as an important event in David's life.

To grasp the reason why, we shall divide the episode
into three parts:
— the census of the people (*vv. 1–9*)
— the punishment (*vv. 10–15*)
— the foreshadowing of the temple, the promise (*vv.
16–25*).

Taken as a whole, what we have here is a mysterious fragment about sin, even if it isn't clear at first sight just what
sin is being dealt with.

The census of the people and David's sin

"Again the anger of the Lord was kindled against Israel
and he incited David against them, saying, 'Go, number
Israel and Judah!' "

The book of *Chronicles* in the parallel chapter (*1
Chron 21*) explains, with its more theological approach,
that it wasn't the anger of the Lord but Satan who

stood up against Israel. Satan it was who prompted David to take a census of the Israelites (*v. 1*).

So what's wrong with taking a census of the people, a civil operation to assess the national resources of manpower? There must be something wrong since Joab's first reaction, absolutely loyal to the king as he is, is to oppose it.

— On the other hand we find other examples of census-taking in the Bible. It is mentioned in *Exodus* as an operation whereby the people can be identified and made aware of their potentialities; in this case indeed emphasis is laid on the sacred nature of the census. Moses says to the Lord: "But now, if thou wilt forgive their sin . . . and if not, blot me, I pray thee, out of thy book which thou hast written!" (*Ex 32:32*). Taking the census is equivalent to entering the number of those who belong to God; he it is who writes the names in the book and he who blots them out.

Hence the sacred quality I mentioned.

— Another passage, also in the book of *Exodus*: "The Lord said to Moses, 'When you take the census of the people of Israel, then each shall give a ransom for himself to the Lord when you number them, that there be no plague among them when you number them' " (*Ex 30:11–12*). Census-taking belongs to God and has to be done with great care, or something may go wrong in the course of it. Rules governing this follow: "Each one who is numbered in the census shall give this: half a shekel according to the shekel of the sanctuary (the shekel is twenty gerahs), half a shekel as an offering to the Lord" (*v. 13*).

This is the sign that life belongs to God and that the people belongs to him too. If anything has to be done affecting the people, this must be done with reverence and respect, since the people is the treasure of the Lord. Hence the sacredness of life is sacredness of the people as a whole, not merely of the individual.

— Another instance of census-taking is to be found in the book of *Numbers*, the numbers being in fact the census figures: "The Lord spoke to Moses in the wilderness of Sinai, in the tent of meeting, on the first day of the second month, in the second year after they had come out of

the land of Egypt, saying, 'Take a census of all the con-
gregation of the people of Israel, by families, by fathers'
houses, according to the number of names, every male, head
by head' " (*Num 1:1–2*).

In Israel therefore census-taking was usual enough, even
if it did have to be conducted with pure hands.

In the West we have lost any sense of this activity's being a sacred one, though other civilisations still preserve it.

In the Bible it is absolutely clear that you cannot touch
the heads of individuals or the people in any way whatever,
without touching something that belongs to God.

— In what then consists David's sin? The operation car-
ried out by Joab and his men is described with great exact-
ness: they start on the far side of the Jordan, then they cover
the south, then the north as far as Sidon. For David, this
is a moment of glory, for never before had Israel occupied
so large a territory.

It seems to me the key to understanding the story lies in
v. 2: "Go through all the tribes of Israel, from Dan to Beersheba, and number the people, *that I may know the number
of the people*".

David doesn't wish to recognise God's ownership but
sees the people of Israel as his own strength, his own
ambition.

In more modern terms we can say that census means
ownership, efficiency, power in David's mind. The humble servant succumbs to the temptation of thinking of
himself as boss, acquires a boss's heart, enters into the spirit
of ownership. He wants to take the measure of his success
— you recall our comments on yesterday's gospel (*) — to
have its secret, to be sure of efficiency.

The result is amazing: Israel numbered eight hundred
thousand men capable of bearing arms, and Judah five hundred thousand. David no longer needs to rely on God, as
he had to do in the days of Goliath, since from now on he's
the most powerful king on earth and can manage on his
own!

(*) See the homily: *The humble economy of the Kingdom*, p. 11.

The punishment

The feeling of power acquired by David is clearly attested by his own words: "After this, David's heart smote him and he said to the Lord, 'I have sinned greatly' " (*v. 10*). He himself perceives his mistake.

It is interesting to observe a parallel at another moment of David's life, when he rejects the opportunity to kill King Saul: "David arose and stealthily cut off the skirt of Saul's robe. And afterwards *David's heart smote him,* because he had cut off Saul's skirt. He said to his men, 'The Lord forbid that I should do this thing to my lord, the Lord's anointed, to put forth my hand against him, seeing he is the Lord's anointed' " (*1 Sam 24:4–6*). He felt he had touched something sacred, had set hands on something belonging to God.

"Now, O Lord, I pray thee, take away the iniquity of thy servant; for I have done very foolishly!" (*2 Sam 24:10*).

The Lord then makes him choose his own punishment and David's reply is very fine: "Let us fall into the hand of the Lord, for his mercy is great" (*v. 14*).

Behold David sinful *yet believing*: awareness of God's mercy is present even in this gloomy turn of events.

What is the Lord's punishment?

It is the exact opposite of the hypnotic dream of success; it is the anguish of total failure. David sees himself dispossessed of his men: seventy thousand of them die.

Instead of effectiveness, he sees the structure of his nation shattered. Instead of power, he feels the utter helplessness of a man confronting the scourge of plague. he realises his own weakness, the uselessness of all human means, and admits to himself that he is at the mercy of unforeseeable circumstances.

And thus he is punished in the three passions that intoxicated him, and gets thoroughly humiliated.

The foreshadowing of the Temple

God's mercy, which David invokes when choosing his

punishment, manifests itself more luminously in the third part of this episode.

The exterminating angel stands with his hand outstretched towards Jerusalem when "the Lord repented of the evil and said to the angel who was working destruction among the people, 'It is enough; now stay your hand' " (*v. 16*). God takes pity on Jerusalem.

"The angel of the Lord was by the threshing floor of Araunah the Jebusite. Then David spoke to the Lord when he saw the angel who was smiting the people, and said, 'Lo, I have sinned, and I have done wickedly, but these sheep – what have they done? Let your hand, I pray thee, be against me and against my father's house' " (*vv. 16–17*).

Once King David says these words, the prophet tells him to build an altar on the Jebusite's threshing floor. David then completes his sacrifice and builds an altar; and this is the beginning of the Temple, since on that very spot Solomon's Temple was to rise, which we still revere in Jerusalem today.

So, from David's human defeat rises the luminous sign of God's presence and infinite mercy.

Application of the story

I have offered you a few pointers but this text is not an easy one to interpret. Many aspects of it are still obscure; the concept of God is pretty rigid, and yet in my view it contains lessons to impress that very primitive soul lurking in each of us when as yet unilluminated by the light of Jesus: for example, a certain fear of provoking God's anger, fear of having handled holy things.

First and foremost however we should ask ourselves what David's temptation means for us today.

The obsession with efficiency, with success, with power, is certainly a *collective* modern temptation, particularly in the Western world.

The Church lives in this atmosphere and is thus drawn to check out the efficacity of its means, of its activities, to make use of methods technologically efficient. Using them isn't bad, if the intention is good; but the idolising of success can easily creep in.

David didn't sin in the carrying out of the census, but in the spirit in which he ordered it. And we ought to be careful: for a praiseworthy exterior action can never — of itself, that is to say — ensure that we perform it with the right disposition.

1) The temptation of success can afflict *churchmen*, hence us, when we give way to the obsession with seeing results, with instant returns; we want other people to recognise how excellent our projects are.

One can actually end up measuring the divine economy by the yardstick of our multinational companies: Why doesn't God help us find more efficient instruments? Perhaps he has deserted us!

To be sure, there are all sorts of tensions within the Church. It is true the Devil has his own job to do, but we may well wonder why he finds it so very easy to do it.

In my view, one of the reasons is that many people in the Church think their own little personal project is God's project. Whence the quarrels, divisions, even schisms.

2) The temptation can afflict *ecclesiastical institutions*, I mean movements, Catholic schools, universities, when self-admiration sets in, or the satisfaction inspired by power or efficiency.

One claims to be at the centre of the Church and ends up despising everyone else.

The initial purpose is good but subsequently everything gets spoilt.

The right way to go about things is by serving the Church, not some group or party label.

I'm thinking, for instance, of all those movements pressing their own activities on the bishop as though they were the key to salvation for the Church and human race at large. And it isn't easy to convince such people that other people too have their keys and that what is needed is for all these various projects to be integrated into a wider frame.

The local Church is precisely that wider frame into which the small contribution of each should be absorbed.

3)   Even so, the temptation is essentially a personal one, manifesting itself as fear of evangelical poverty, in complaints about not having what seems needed. The complaint may be perfectly justified; often however it is resentful and linked to the sin of David: if I had more, I should succeed; I could depend on my own resources.

Conclusion

In conclusion I want to emphasise that success does have an importance of its own and is a part of our work. I shouldn't at all like you to fall into the opposite extreme of seeking failure for its own sake, for equilibrium is a characteristic of Catholicism. Jesus himself wanted his preaching to be well received. Human satisfaction is hence a good and not an evil thing, and biblical spirituality teaches as much.

A sense of proportion though is essential, a scale of values, the scale David temporarily lost sight of.

Whoever puts God first: "O God, thou art my God", has nothing to fear. If I have chosen God as my supreme good, from whom no force in the world — neither life nor death, nor sickness, nor defeat — can detach me, the rest will look after itself.

The ultimate good is God communicating himself to us and the ultimate goods therefore are grace, prayer, charity. This primacy once in place, come the penultimate goods, the foregoing reflected in history: friendship, joy, loyalty, faithfulness, righteousness, love, togetherness. And the praeter-penultimate good things, constituting the natural *desiderata* for the others, are health, food, work, success, good results, satisfaction.

So you see success too has its place in the scheme of things.

What the Lord wants is the inner order reigning in David's heart when he sang *Psalm 63*.

We can desire the praeter-penultimate good things, we can strive to get them and complain when they don't arrive, all the while knowing however that the ultimate good things are something else.

And I think that, not in theory but certainly in daily practice, the order the Lord wishes is unclear. Hence let us pray:

'O Lord, show me the element of disorder, of confusion, within me. Purify my heart, order my desires, rectify my intentions, so that I may choose you first of all, Supreme Good, and so that I may see all the other good things needful to me and others, for which we have to work. Lord, all earthly things are lovely, but in that order of love that Jesus teaches us — that you, Jesus, our Messiah, true man and true God, teach us by your death and resurrection.'

TRUE KINSHIP

(Homily for Tuesday in the XVI week "per annum")

The gospel passage that has just been read is taken from *Matthew 12:46–50*. Even as regards its setting it isn't easy to understand.

Jesus it seems is in a house, since it says that his mother and brothers are "outside" and aren't able to talk to him.

Even so, Jesus "was still talking to the people" and it is impossible to imagine how the crowd could be in a confined space. Possibly a small group is meant, just a few people. In yesterday's passage it was the scribes and Pharisees who were questioning the Master. So in this room let us try to envisage Jesus, his disciples seated round him, with a handful of scribes, Pharisees and other people as well.

Such is the scene.

Outside the door there are a great many people, among whom are Mary and other relatives, crowding round; they keep sending in messages; eventually someone inside hears and says to Jesus: "I say, your mother and brothers are outside, wanting to talk to you". Jesus replies: " 'Who is my mother and who are my brothers?' And stretching out his hand towards his disciples, he said, 'Here are my mother and my brothers! For whoever does the will of my Father in heaven is my brother, and sister, and mother'."

We can understand he might not want to talk to his brothers but we cannot at all understand the meaning of his refusal to speak to his own mother.

As we know, this is not an isolated passage. There is another, harsher one that occurs uniquely in Mark's gospel (*3:20–21*). Jesus's relatives (his mother isn't mentioned) come to take charge of him, having heard that he couldn't even have a meal; they say: "He is beside himself" (*v. 21*). One may well suppose these are the same relatives as those written of by Matthew.

Another text strikes much the same note: the twelve-year-old Jesus has just been discovered in the Temple and Mary says to him: "Your father and I have been looking for you". Jesus replies: "How is it that you sought me? Did you not know that I must be in my Father's house?" (*Lk 2:48–49*).

On the same lines, I should mention the incident of the marriage at Cana, when Jesus turns to his Mother with these words: "Woman, what have you to do with me?" (*Jn 2:4*).

So, you see Jesus's answer is not an isolated one and we must discover what *message* it contains.

1) A first meaning of the message is that *the ties of fleshly relationship take second place to those of spiritual relationship*. This was a totally revolutionary criterion for Israel, as indeed for any other civilisation. All life begins from physical relationship which is the well-spring of all brotherhood, and society is based on this factual datum. So, for instance, the ancient philosophers like Cicero recognised that charity was none other than the diffusion towards others of that love which one feels towards one's nearest and dearest. And this charity is true righteousness.

In Jesus's world, physical relationship was fundamental and on it depended one's religion, starting with Abraham and down through all his descendants.

Now, Jesus doesn't deny being a son of David, but explains the true significance of this: physical relationship is, as it were, the reference point for a deeper understanding.

2) The second meaning of the message is that true kinship depends on the *will of God*. This affirmation is also found in the Koran. A Koranic scholar came to visit us at the Biblical Institute, I remember, and we discussed our respective Sacred Books. At the end, he quoted me a verse of the Prophet's which says something more or less like this: Studying the Bible makes kin of all who work hard at it.

Spiritual relationship which is born of study of the Book, for Jesus is born, more profoundly, of the will of God, the will of the Father.

We glimpse the outline of a society based on ties born of human decision and God's decision, not merely on ties unquestioningly received.

3) It follows that in the Kingdom of God *there are no privileges other than those conferred by the Father's will.*

There are no privileges of blood, of family, and this is very hard to grasp. Even today the Jews haven't managed to grasp it, since for them descent from Abraham means physical descent.

Mary understood this however and she accepted it.

4) A last meaning is that *Jesus is* presented as *the definitive messiah*, re-organising all life's other values in relation to himself: "Whoever does the will of my Father in heaven is my brother, and sister, and mother".

The supreme value is God, communicating himself in Jesus, and Jesus creates a new order of values.

We understand this well enough with our heads but do not so often succeed in putting it into practice. If we think about it carefully, it ought to be the principle of community life; the will of God is what makes us brothers and sisters in the religious life. The community is thus dependent on faith, on the degree of faith with which we have really entrusted ourselves to the will of the Father.

From this it follows that a religious community is a community living its life according to the gospel, not an entity working to its own rules. A family, by virtue of the very diversity of temperaments and characters composing it, has an almost physical strength holding it together. In the religious life, that force is faith, and if faith is weak the harsh demands of the common life will be extremely hard to meet.

The difficulties we experience in our own community, and in every Christian community, originate from a lack of total dedication to Jesus; consequently relationships remain superficial, the brotherly life is lived by act of will, not with the heart, and we don't communicate, don't open up; that loving devotion making everything joyous and easy is not to be found.

This is no small problem in the Church.

Similarly, in the missions I have visited in Asia, Africa and Latin America, I have been struck by the endless arguments among the missionaries, among Christians. And yet here we have men and women who have left all, who have performed the heroic act of setting out for distant lands and who should in consequence find themselves in a deeply brotherly relationship with one another. This however isn't the case.

Certainly there's a mystery here, incomprehensible but none the less real.

If on the one hand we ought not to be too surprised about this, on the other we ought on no account to get accustomed to it. For it is bad, it is abnormal, it is not right; every day we must force ourselves to enter into the heart of Jesus so as to allow him to change our hearts; every day we must implore him to increase our faith.

During this Eucharist, let us pray over all the mistakes we have committed against brotherly love, all the times we have not looked on the brothers and sisters as real brothers and sisters to whom everything can sincerely and joyfully be forgiven. Jesus is brother, sister and mother to us and becomes this to those who live with us, who share our ideals about life, who support us along the common path.

'Forgive us, Lord, our divisions; heal our wounds and inner divisions. Grant us that peace that comes from you and is the sign that we are one and one alone in you.'

4

Carelessness over small matters

Let us now consider David's second sin, emphasised in the Bible, while we meditate on the theme of *Psalm 51* stated in its title: *To the choirmaster. A psalm of David, when Nathan the prophet came to him, after he had gone in to Bathsheba.*

"Have mercy on me, O God, according to your steadfast love; according to your abundant mercy blot out my transgressions. Wash me thoroughly from my iniquity and cleanse me from my sin. For I know my transgressions" (*Ps 51:1–3*).

'*Grant me, O God, to acknowledge my sin just as David acknowledged his. Grant that the Virgin Mary may obtain for me, as St Ignatius suggests in the third exercise of the first week* (cf n. 63), *three graces: to have an interior knowledge of my sins and a detestation of them. To be aware of the disorder within me so that I may order myself aright; David says that you love truth in the inward being and that you can teach me wisdom in my secret heart* (cf Ps 51:8). *Teach me this order and, lastly, as third grace, give me knowledge of the world so that I may reject whatever is vain. Give me therefore knowledge of the circumstantial things of life, of the little things that are causes of great errors. Do not let me regard small defects as commonplace and negligible. Purge me, my God, with hyssop and I shall be clean; wash me and I shall be whiter than snow. Fill me once more with joy and gladness and let the bones which thou has broken rejoice* (cf Ps 51:9–10).'

David's second sin is in fact recounted first in the Scriptures and we read of it in the *Second Book of Samuel* at chapter 11.

The structure of David's spirituality

The passage (*2 Sam 11:2–27*) is one of the masterpieces of Biblical literature and, while we meditate on it, we should note the wonderful psychological analysis of David's heart made in it.

I leave it to you to read it through very slowly, and confine myself to underlining a few details by way of reflecting on *carelessness over small matters*.

My suggestions are made towards providing an answer to the question: how on earth could the overlooking of a few trivialities amounting to carelessness have led David to become the very opposite of all he was?

We've already said he was certainly a sinner, not a saint; even so, a man with principles he never repudiated, with a well defined spiritual structure of his own.

He was, that is to say, loyal, faithful unto death as regards his friends, capable of respecting oaths and the rules of war as it was then waged.

1) Let us think for instance of the various passages describing the deep sense of friendship he cherished for Jonathan, the son of his enemy. Even after Jonathan's death, David was to ask: "Is there still anyone left of the house of Saul, that I may show him kindness for Jonathan's sake?" (*2 Sam 9:1*). This loyalty, by which he set more store than anything else, gave David his great stature in his people's eyes.'

2) He was cruel but respected the rules of war. Those two moments come to mind when he could have killed King Saul but refrained out of respect for the Lord's anointed and because it would have been dishonourable to kill an enemy by treachery (cf *1 Sam 24:26*).

3) Another marvellous example, making David the most attractive of Old Testament heroes, is his lament for Saul and Jonathan, his truly sincere grief over the king's death. The elegy he utters reveals a heart completely loyal to the man who, had he been able, would gladly have wiped his name off the earth. I quote these few lines from it:

"Saul and Jonathan, beloved and lovely!
   In life and in death they were not divided;
they were swifter than eagles,
   they were stronger than lions.

Ye daughters of Israel, weep over Saul,
   who clothed you daintily in scarlet,
   who put ornaments of gold upon your apparel.

How are the mighty fallen
   in the midst of the battle!

Jonathan lies slain upon thy high places.
   I am distressed for you, my brother Jonathan;
very pleasant have you been to me." (*2 Sam 1:23f*)

Chapter 11 however describes the stages of a process in which, through small and insignificant circumstances, the hero David becomes *disloyal, unfaithful, treacherous*. If anyone had said, that day he went for a stroll on the terrace: Look out or you'll be murdering your best friend, the man more loyal to you than any other, he would certainly have replied: That couldn't possibly happen.

The history of a sin

"At the time when kings go forth to battle, David sent Joab, and his servants with him, and all Israel, and they ravaged the Ammonites and besieged Rabbah" (*2 Sam 11:1*). David no longer imposes the arduous business on himself of going forth to war; he is content with his royal throne, he doesn't take the risks he used to. We can say he now feels sure of himself. This first verse sets the scene for what follows.

With great psychological finesse the writer notes that it all began with a mere *inquisitive glance*: "It happened, late one afternoon, when David arose from his couch and was walking on the roof of the king's house, that he saw from the roof a woman bathing; and the woman was very beautiful" (*v. 2*). Why on earth did he look at her? Probably because he thought that, being old and full of experience, it was all right for him to do so: simple curiosity which couldn't have any consequences for a man like him.

The second incident is an *imprudence*: "David sent and inquired about the woman. And someone said, Is not this Bathsheba, daughter of Eliam and wife of Uriah the Hittite?" (*v. 3*).

Again it's a matter of very minor importance and David has no notion of what may develop from it.

Now the imprudence becomes more serious: "Then David sent messengers and took her" (*v. 4a*).

Wishing to excuse him, we may think he was merely acting on a whim. He only wanted to make her acquaintance, nothing more: to bring her to court to lend a hand with the housework.

The truth was, he'd already made up his mind.

Now the text gathers speed: "She came to him and he lay with her. (Now she was purifying herself from her uncleanness.) Then she returned to her house. And the woman conceived; and she sent and told David, I am with child" (*vv. 4–5*).

From glance to pregnancy — everything unfolds as in a dream.

And this is where the real story of David's sin begins. Up to this point one can talk about weakness, stupidity, vanity: he believed himself to be strong, above such trifles. But now the problem has to be faced. What is to be done?

To begin with, David thinks: I shall get myself out of this embarrassing situation, I shall do all I can to save my own reputation and the woman's honour; it's an awkward situation but I shall get out of it.

Sure of himself, "he sent word to Joab, 'Send me Uriah the Hittite.' And Joab sent Uriah to David. When Uriah came to him, David asked how Joab was doing, and how the people fared and how the war prospered" (*vv. 6–7*). He pretends nothing is wrong, tries to flatter Uriah by emphasising his soldierly talents, and so becomes deceitful.

Then as though *en passant*, " 'Go down to your house and wash your feet.' And Uriah went out of the king's house, and there followed him a present from the king. But Uriah slept at the door of the king's house with all the servants of his lord and did not go down to his house" (*vv. 8–9*). Perhaps Uriah had twigged; perhaps David's tone of voice had given the game away. Or perhaps he hadn't understood anything at all and was merely observing the rules of war.

On this first night, the king begins to realise things aren't going to be as easy as he had supposed; he can't control the situation as he had imagined. Even so, he doesn't discard his domineering manner.

"When they told David, Uriah did not go down to his house, David said to Uriah: 'Have you not come from a journey? Why did you not go down to your house?' Uriah said to David: 'The ark and Israel and Judah dwell in booths; and my lord Joab and the servants of my lord are camping in the open fields; shall I then go to my house, to eat and to drink, and to lie with my wife? As you live and as your soul lives, I will not do this thing' " (*vv. 10–11*).

The passage is full of irony and one gets the distinct impression Uriah is making fun of the king, as though he has his suspicions and is hoping to trip him up. David for his part, in his confusion, tries to beguile the man with his kindness and hospitality, while Uriah, upsetting his flow, takes his stand on loyalty, respect for God and the rules of war. It is a battle of wits and the king gets the worst of it.

He doesn't however mean to admit defeat and so he invites Uriah to drink and eat in his presence, eventually getting him drunk. Even when drunk, Uriah still won't go home and sleeps with the servants.

During this terrible night, for the first time David realises he has become his own prisoner.

Even so, he doesn't say; What have I done? His mind is entirely set on one thing: how to save three objects on which he sets great value, by which he is ensnared:

— the first is the *good reputation of the king*;

— The second is the *mother*, with the child, whom he wants to live at all cost. He could have abandoned the woman, knowing she would have let herself be put to death

rather than tell her husband the name of the man who had made her pregnant; he loves her however and does not want to lose her;
— the third is his friend Uriah, whom he can't afford to get rid of.

He doesn't know what to do. Let the king's reputation be ruined? Out of the question. Let the woman and child die. No way. Get rid of his friend? No.

He goes from one thing he prizes to the next, unwilling to give up any one of them. This is the sin, the disorder: the arrival due to carelessness, lack of attention, super-ficiality, at a situation becoming more insoluble by the minute.

Perhaps, for the first time in his life, David feels afraid, realising he will be forced to renounce one of the three things he values. He spends the whole night arguing with himself; by dawn he is exhausted. On the spur of the moment he decides: he will sacrifice his friend.

Cunningly, perfidiously but perhaps already with a broken heart, he writes a letter to Joab and sends Uriah to deliver it: "In the letter he wrote: Set Uriah in the forefront of the hardest fighting and then draw back from him, so that he may be struck down and die. And as Joab was besieging the city, he assigned Uriah to the place where he knew there were valiant men. And the men of the city came out and fought with Joab; and some of the servants of David among the people fell. Uriah the Hittite was slain also" (*vv. 15–17*).

The story isn't over, for David's sin has very serious consequences. The following verses too are a marvel of the narrative art: the people make fun of the king, they under-stand perfectly well what has happened, and the good reputation David was so desperately anxious to preserve is lost. The ultra-loyal Joab is the first to let the cat out of the bag. He sends the king an account of the battle and says to the messenger: "When you have finished telling all the news . . . if the king's anger rises and if he says to you: 'Why did you go so near the city to fight? Did you not know that they would shoot from the wall? Who killed Abimelech the son of Jerubbesheth? Did not a woman cast an upper millstone upon him from the wall, so that he died at Thebez? Why did you go so near the wall?' then you shall say, 'Your servant Uriah the Hittite is dead also' " (*v. 24*).

Everything went as Joab had foreseen and the narrative proceeds slowly so that we can appreciate every detail. The messenger sets out, then arrives and delivers his message to the king. David falls into a rage and the messenger explains how the battle had gone, and ends up: "Your servant Uriah the Hittite is dead also" (*v. 24*).

Whereupon David says to him: "Thus shall you say to Joab: Do not let this matter trouble you, for the sword devours now one and now another; strengthen your attack upon the city and overthrow it. And encourage him" (*v. 25*).

David stays shut up in his sin, convinced he couldn't have acted differently, justifying himself to himself.

This is the end to which all come who fall short in loyalty to friendship, to family; they do not want to do evil but have no other way of escaping from what they conceive to be a vicious circle.

Now the king has no more scruples about taking Uriah's wife, precisely because he thinks he has done the only right thing possible. Bathsheba becomes David's wife and gives birth to a son.

God guides David towards repentance (2 Samuel 12:1–14)

Chapter 11 ends with a sentence that turns the situation on its head: "But the thing that David had done displeased the Lord" (*v. 27b*).

In fact, the king had completely forgotten about God and the songs he had composed in his honour: "O God, thou art my God . . . I thirst for thee . . . Thou art my rock and my fortress".

Throughout this agonising story it never says once that he prayed. It never entered his head to plead: Lord, help me to get out of this!

He was convinced the problem was his alone and that no one, not even God, could help him. David was thus

profoundly alienated from that spirit of faith, humility and
self-surrender properly his. Probably too he may have
thought: The Lord let me get into this mess; he is no longer
with me.

Sin had brought him to confusion, aridity, sorrow. One
small disorder cultivated had led him to commit one mistake
after another.

With chapter 12, God resumes control of the story: "The
Lord sent the prophet Nathan to David" (*v. 1*). If he hadn't
sent him, David would have remained convinced for the rest
of his life that he had made the only possible choice.

The Lord however desires order, peace, truth, as it is written in *Psalm 51:6*: "Thou desirest truth in the inward
being".

The narrative continues with a parable and this by degrees
restructures truth in David: "There were two men in a certain city, the one rich and the other poor. The rich man
had very many flocks and herds; but the poor man had
nothing but one little ewe lamb, which he had bought. And
he brought it up, and it grew up with him and with his
children; it used to eat of his morsel, and drink from his
cup, and lie in his bosom, and it was like a daughter to him.
Now there came a traveller to the rich man, and he was unwilling to take one of his own flock or herd to prepare for
the wayfarer who had come to him, but he took the poor
man's lamb, and prepared it for the man who had come
to him" (*12:1–4*).

The style is bald, a bit ingenuous, since it deals with an
extreme situation.

David repents. God in his infinite goodness and
psychological subtilty sets him free by seizing on his own
best qualities: his loyalty and his need to defend the right.
The prophet doesn't haul him over the coals, as we might
do in a case of this sort. If Nathan had taken him to task,
he would probably argued back that he was justified in doing what he did. The appeal however isn't made to David
the sinner but to David the just, the loyal, and this is why
it succeeds: "David's anger was greatly kindled against the
man; and he said to Nathan, 'As the Lord lives, the

man who has done this deserves to die; and he shall restore
the lamb fourfold, because he did this thing, and because
he had no pity' " (*vv. 5–6*).

Now comes the trickiest moment of all: what is Nathan
to say? Will he have the guts to speak out? We know from
experience how hard it can be having to face certain situations and how often we lack courage to tell the truth.
"Nathan said to David, 'You are the man. Thus says the
Lord, the God of Israel, "I anointed you king over Israel,
and I delivered you out of the hand of Saul; and I gave you
your master's house, and your master's wives into your
bosom, and gave you the house of Israel and of Judah; and
if this were too little, I would add to you as much more.
Why have you despised the word of the Lord, to do what
is evil in his sight?" ' " (*vv. 7–9*).

David is struck to the heart and confesses his guilt to
Nathan, having heard God's punishment from his lips. "I
have sinned against the Lord" (v. 13). Now he regains all
his spiritual stature, he throws off the terrible incubus and
realises what the simpler, more obvious way of escape would
have been: renouncing his own respectability to affirm the
supremacy of God. Having meant to defend the privileges
of the throne, he has entered on a series of lies, a course
of disloyalty, culminating in murder. His own admission
is born of a sincere and humbled heart. Nathan tells him
that the Lord forgives him and will spare his life. Instead
the child born of Bathsheba shall die.

Recognising ourselves in David

Replete with wisdom, there is nothing remote about this
story where we are concerned, for David is a great model
for all ages.

From it we learn how by small acts of carelessness we
can find ourselves in serious difficulties, and how if we do
not keep our gaze fixed on God we fall into ever worse
errors in attempting to cover those that have gone before.
Yet God is rich in mercy and intervenes to help us rediscover
the best in ourselves, to rediscover those gifts the Holy Spirit

has put in our hearts: love of truth, love of justice, love of loyalty.

The words of Jesus admonish us today and every day: "Out of the heart come evil thoughts, murder, adultery, fornication, theft, false witness, slander. These are what defile a man" (*Mt 15:19*).

We recognise ourselves in David because in every one of us there is that wicked heart from which disorder comes.

This is why *Psalm 51* and this story invite us to reflect seriously: merely because we are not king or do not have David's power, we cannot presume that we are exempt from guilt.

Our human condition is fated to disorder and hence we run the risk, at least in trivial matter, of becoming prisoners of ourselves, unable to recognise and confess that we are sinners.

God's grace alone, continually invoked and awaited, can bring us back each day to the truth.

5

David's confession

'O God our Father who understood the heart of David, grant us so to understand that human heart as to understand our own and the heart of your Son Jesus.

Virgin Mary, daughter of Sion, who gave birth to the Saviour, grant us to understand his heart, the better to understand our own hearts and the hearts of those we love, of those entrusted to us and, above all, of those who suffer and those who live without hope.

Grant us a sense of time: of the past, of the present and of the future. Teach us to be aware of the disorder in our lives so that we may make ourselves to the dimensions of God's time, the time of mercy and love.

We ask this of you, Father, for the sake of your Son Jesus, in the Holy Spirit, in union with Mary. Amen'.

The messianic outcome to David's sins

Today, and still in the spirit of the first week of St Ignatius's *Exercises*, we shall more specifically meditate on *Psalm 51*. First however I should like you to note that those two sins of David's over which we have lingered have each a *messianic outcome*; and this no doubt is why the Bible lays so much emphasis on these two sinful actions of the king's.

We should accustom ourselves, while reading the story of David, to observing the way the events are interwoven, little by little to form a single design expanding into the revelation of Jesus.

— The sin of the census-taking, as we have said, concludes with the prefiguring of the Temple: by way of guilt, punishment, angel and Jerusalem, we come to see the first altar, the sign of God's presence among his people, the

beginning of that Temple which was to prefigure the
ultimate Temple, Jesus with us, Emmanuel.

— The adultery with Bathsheba and the murder of Uriah
lead to the birth of Solomon, the ante-type of the Prince
of Peace.

If you read the opening words of the New Testament,
you will see that all this was perfectly clear to the mind of
the sacred writer: "Genealogy of Jesus Christ, the son of
David, the son of Abraham . . . David was the father of
Solomon by the wife of Uriah"(cf *Mt 1:1ff*). Bathsheba is
identified as being Uriah's wife, precisely to recall the grim
events leading up to Solomon's birth.

Not only her: for in this gospel passage three other women
are named: Tamar, Rahab and Ruth, all of them connected
with significant events whether more or less edifying — in
sacred history. This is as much as to say that Jesus in himself
sums up the memories of the past, which hence are not to
be forgotten.

We are called to know *this* Jesus, who is the Messiah of
the human race.

Going back to David, I suggest you reflect on the entire
context in which the story of Bathsheba and Uriah is set,
asking yourselves in prayer why the Holy Scriptures made
a point of relating such events and devoted so much space
to describing this particular sin of David's and attaching
so much importance to the royal succession (cf *1 Kings*).
Only by doing this, will you be able to understand the figure
of David in its full significance and, in consequence, understand the course of salvation-history, and understand then
that in the countenance of Christ shine forth the light of
God and hope of mankind.

We shall have more to say on this topic later.

Psalm 51

For me, and no doubt for you, the *"Miserere"* is full of
memories; for me, it gives rise to different emotions every
time I read it.

In the pastoral year 1982–1983 I proposed it to the young

people of the Diocese of Milan for the meetings of the *Scuola della Parola*, the transactions of which were later transcribed and published in book form; as a result of this, I received a very beautiful re-write of the psalm from a terrorist locked up in one of the city gaols. The *"Miserere"* does indeed have an extraordinary capacity for piercing the human heart and on this point alone it would be hard to comment in a single meditation.

Even so, in itself, it is extremely simple, the nub of it being the words that David said to Nathan: "I have sinned against the Lord" (*2 Sam 12:13*).

This being once established, it isn't of so much importance to know whether the *"Miserere"* was composed by David personally, or composed later and based on David's story.

True, it reveals a profound relationship with the prophetic books, particularly with Isaiah and Ezekiel. For instance *v. 7*: "Purge me with hyssop and I shall be clean; wash me and I shall be whiter than snow", has much in common with the prophet's penitential prayer: "Come now, let us reason together, says the Lord: though your sins are like scarlet, they shall be as white as snow" (*Is 1:18*).

Again, *v. 10*: "Create in me a clean heart, O God" recalls Ezekiel: "I will give them a new heart and put a new spirit within them" (*Ezek 11:19*).

The *Jerusalem Bible* lists all the other references to the prophets.

One might read the psalm as expressing the religious emotions of a people at a given point in its history. We however shall apply it to any individual who recognises his or her disordered state before God.

It isn't easy to analyse it, composed as it is like a symphony — of the heart — repeating themes already stated. Even so, *four movements* may be descried in it: the past, the present, the appeal, the future. Let's see what the key-words for each movement are.

The psalm's four movements

1)   First of all, the *past*, consisting of David's words:

"I have sinned". These are repeated in *v. 4*: "Against thee, thee only, have I sinned, and done that which is evil in thy sight".

The verbs are in the past tense and it is particularly interesting to note the structure of this man's confession, as he admits having fallen into disorder. The past is evoked, though very briefly.

2) The *present* is treated a little more diffusely. We read for instance at *v. 3*: "I know my transgressions, and my sin is ever before me".

The nouns used in the various translations to indicate disorder, rebellion, sin, don't do justice to the original language. In the Hebrew text, four words are used to express the states of which David is aware: *pesha', 'awon, hatta, ra'ah.* They mean deviation from the right path, as though one were proceeding in a zig-zag fashion, constantly going to extremes, a kind of mental confusion; then a wicked, spiteful, rebellious, envious, sly heart; disharmony in life, lack of suppleness and equilibrium; the opposite of what is good, the forsaking of good. Various words but all of them indicating the psalmist's awareness of not managing to keep on the right path all the time as he should, of not being at harmony with himself, with God, with nature, with his fellow-beings, of not being kindly disposed but of giving himself over to base thoughts.

3) The *appeal* is a theme occurring right at the beginning and continually recurring throughout. It is a prayer, a plea, a pleading to be purified. The verbs are all in the imperative:

"Have mercy on me, O God, in thy steadfast love,
in thy abundant mercy blot out my transgressions,
wash me thoroughly from my iniquity,
cleanse me from my sin . . .
Purge me with hyssop . . .
Wash me . . .
Fill me with joy and gladness . . .
Hide thy face from my sins . . .
Create in me a clean heart and put a right spirit within me."

This appeal is, first and foremost, full of faith. The psalm is not only a confession of personal guilt but, starting out from this awareness, becomes trust in God, expressed in every possible metaphor:

"Fill me with joy and gladness, let the bones which thou hast broken rejoice!"

In expressing this desire, the psalmist leans on the mercy of God and is thus mysteriously reconstructed.

— *Trust* is the dominant theme of the invocation, first stated in *v. 1*: "Have mercy on me, O God, according to thy steadfast love; according to thy abundant mercy blot out my transgressions".

The Hebrew appeals to God's *hesed*, the fountainhead of all salvation-history. The appeal is based on the first principle and foundation: God loves human beings.

It is striking that the confession should begin with this deep sense of trust, with praise for God, with the proclaiming of his goodness; later comes expression of the shame David feels.

So this is the kind of confession opening the heart, speaking of hope.

By no means does it begin with an excuse. When we ask someone to forgive us, we usually begin like this: I didn't intend to hurt you, I didn't mean to do it, I'm sorry but I didn't think you'd mind . . .

But David, with his first word, appeals to the goodness and tenderness of "his" God, without propping himself up with excuses or expressions of regret.

This is a striking reversal of the norm, since people are always tempted to excuse themselves to God and to claim they're brokenhearted and upset at what they've done.

In the psalm, there is talk of broken bones but only after proclaiming the greatness of God's love.

Trust is therefore a decisive point in the process of confession.

— A second theme of the appeal is the *desire to be purified*: "Wash me . . cleanse me . . purge me . . wash me . . hide thy face from my sins . . blot out . . deliver me from blood-guilt . ."

This desire doesn't stem from human effort but is aroused by God himself.

He doesn't say: I mean to be careful, I don't intend to be negligent any more. He says: wash me, purge me, deliver me because you alone can do it, your mercy alone can make a new man of me.

— Finally, in the appeal we find the notion of *newness*: "Create in me a clean heart, O God" (*v. 10*).

The verb *to create* designates a divine action, God's great action in the beginning when "God created the heavens and the earth ..." (*Gen 1:1f*). Trust in newness of life in the Spirit is extremely important. One of my saddest experiences has been to realise that our society is convinced, for instance, that there is no possibility of a change of heart in those who have committed serious crimes: I'm thinking of people imprisoned for robbery, drug-trafficking, terrorism and so forth. People don't believe human nature can change, they don't believe in real conversion, don't believe that the action of the Spirit can transform hearts and situations.

This lack of hope in others and sometimes in ourselves is a serious matter: "I'm always the same. I shall never change. There's nothing to be done about it". This is the Enemy tempting us into a cynical hopelessness, whereas the *"Miserere"* makes one feel the opposite: "Create in me a clean heart, O God, and put a *right spirit* within me".

In the Old Latin version, the second part of this verse was translated: *Et spiritu principali confirma me*. The *"spiritus principalis"* is invoked on bishops at the moment of their ordination, as the Church also invokes the Holy Spirit on them.

The Hebrew word isn't easy to translate but suggests a sound spirit, serving for a well constructed building.

"Cast me not away from thy presence, and take not thy holy spirit from me; restore to me the joy of thy salvation and uphold me with a willing spirit" (*vv. 11–12*).

The Spirit is mentioned three times, for the Spirit it is that makes the heart new, the Spirit being the gift of the New Testament which renews the human heart.

Very appositely, the *Jerusalem Bible* refers, at *v. 11* ("thy holy spirit") to *Romans 8:9*. The whole of *Romans 8* however, dealing with Christian life according to the Spirit, is suitable for meditation with *Psalm 51*.

4) The fourth theme of the *"Miserere"* is the *future*, treated from *v. 13* onwards:

"I will teach transgressors thy ways
and sinners will return to thee . . .
my tongue will sing aloud of thy deliverance . . .
my mouth shall show forth thy praise."

Here is the hope, appropriate to the new heart, that the future will be different. No longer will it be, as the past was, under the weight of sin, of disorder, of ambition, of life's futility. Rather it will be directed towards mission, the apostolate, the preaching to all and sundry about a change of heart: "I will teach transgressors thy ways". Not only shall I get back on my feet, I shall help others too.

How amazingly rich this psalm is, enchanting us alike with the breadth of sentiment it evokes and the tenderness, sagacity and psychological subtilty of the words. In them are mirrored every bad and every good emotion in the human heart.

Awareness of sin and of dimensions of time

I should like to conclude with one observation.

The four movements — past, present, appeal, future — mean that awareness of sin, in the presence of divine mercy, reveals the different dimensions of time to us.

Our own time, often turned in on a boring, difficult, vexatious present, opens up as soon as we become aware of our disorder and hence completely aware of the real situation. The past is never to be forgotten, for it makes its appeal for mercy in the present, in sure and certain hope of the future.

For this reason, it's sad when people are afraid of sacramental confession and do not care to complete the journey, so renouncing the spiritual largesse that flows from the purifying process.

Confession isn't something painful, obligatory, formal;

it helps us to appropriate to ourselves the temporal dimensions of our lives without denying anything; it helps us to incorporate those less satisfactory feelings of ours which we normally try to marginalise, by expressing them to God. Confession, I insist, is a true way of liberation, an absolutely necessary one.

Hence I suggest you try to make your confession by basing yourself on the experience of the psalmist, by putting *praise of God* in first place, affirmation of his love and tenderness, of the marvels he has wrought in your life.

Then the heart will open, reaffirming time past and present, making us *confess what we are*, telling God about those deep-down feelings — the things that get on our nerves, our worries, feelings of resentment, of disgust, enmities — which weigh on us and are the root of so many shortcomings.

At this point, the *confession of faith* begins, the plea to be set free, purged of what we do not wish to be; to be changed: "create in me a new heart, O God, grant me the joy of your salvation, do not deprive me of your holy spirit, for it will not be the scale of my repentance but your love that will transform my life!" This, the prayer that gently leads us into Christ's mercy, that mercy descending on us in the sacrament of penance.

THE PARABLES: AN EXAMPLE OF PATIENCE
(Homily for Wednesday in the XVI week "per annum")

'Why, Jesus, did you speak in parables? You know God better than any of us, you are the Son of God and could speak openly, directly about him. Why didn't you do so? Why didn't you clearly explain the mystery of God and the mystery of mankind?'
The gospel passage for today offers us the parable of the sower (*Mt 13:1–9*). The problem of the parables vexed even the evangelists themselves and in tomorrow's gospel we shall see a possible key to its solution.

Today however I am particularly anxious to emphasise that Jesus spoke in parables to set us an *example of patience*.

We always get impatient when there's talk of the mystery of God and the mystery of mankind; we should like exact, watertight definitions. But this would be lacking respect for God, the mystery of whom is very deep, and for the human personality too, since this is not to be known as you might a stone.

It's hard enough to know all about a stone, a tree, an animal organism; how much harder to know all there is to know about a man or woman.

He who truly knows the mystery of God keeps silent: this is what Jesus did. He could have revealed all — and the apocryphal gospels credit him with all sorts of secret revelations made to his disciples — but for thirty years he said nothing.

Before the mystery of God therefore we are invited to adore, to respect, to stand in silence.

Before the mystery of mankind, we can only cherish an attitude of great reverence, since our knowledge cannot be other than approximate.

In the parables, Jesus teaches us to speak about the mysteries of God and mankind by approximations, with successive comparisons, without ever giving us a homogeneous frame — to make us realise they remain beyond the scope of any explanation.

It may happen to you and it certainly does to me, especially during a course of Exercises, to feel a sense of shame
after the meditation, on perceiving that what I have said
is not the mystery of God: it is it and it is not it.

A parable has this same progression: it is thus, at the same
time it is not. This appeals to that deep intuition which is
the Holy Spirit within us. The Holy Spirit is within us as
he was in Jesus and spoke in him.

And so it is the Holy Spirit who grants us intuition of
the mystery.

And the Spirit it is, within me and within those listening
to me, who gives meaning to this "beyond" to which I have
recourse in the poverty of my own words. Sometimes inef-
fectiveness and uncertainty in preaching indicates the need
for a return to that mystery which is always beyond.

The thing to do then is surrender oneself to the Spirit and
accept definitions of the faith as signposts. Naturally, there
are precise formulae to define the faith, but they don't
express the reality.

Thus, the most perfect formula — the Father, the Son,
the Holy Spirit; the Son who took flesh and died for us —
cannot convey the movement, the energy of the mystery.

Only the Holy Spirit can give us the intuition and let us
actually handle what words express as signs to mark the
way.

This is why, I think, Jesus loved parables. Because, knowing the Father, he knew he couldn't speak directly about
him, and the best way of giving an idea of the Father was
to start from the familiar things of life: fishing, farming,
work, family, meals, festivals, weddings, friendship. In these
realities is revealed an impulse — a progress beyond —
towards that which is most transcendent in human experience and derived from God, that is to say, his grace.

The transcendent is clothed in a parable, so as to draw
us beyond ourselves, towards the beginning and end of all.

Our prayer before Jesus, speaker in parables, should be:

*'Out of the depths I call to you, Lord. You who dwell
in the heights, free me from my commonplace and*

superficial interpretation of the world. Cause me, Lord, to understand the strength of the Spirit sown in the soil of the world, to have faith in this world, to have faith in the energy dwelling in the universe and allow myself to be drawn by it towards the depths of the Father, to give myself to the Son by allowing myself to be enfolded in the Spirit's embrace which will open the wellsprings of life within me.

Grant me, Lord, to grasp what the parable is, to read the parable of life, of history, of my own life, and to see you, Lord, as you have promised us; to know you as we are known; to gaze at you, no longer through a veil, an enigma, a mirror, but directly, and to begin contemplating you now with the eye of faith. Grant me to fasten my contemplation on this good seed dwelling on earth and transforming it: the Eucharist, which is placed in the soil of the world and yields a hundredfold in the hearts that receive it in faith and humility.'

6

David and Christology

'We worship and glorify you, Almighty Father, rich in grace and mercy.

Help us to know and understand your Son Jesus as the Messiah, son of David, heir to his throne, King of kings, Lord of lords, so as to love and worship him as God and follow him as the Saviour of mankind.

Grant that by gazing on him in contemplation, we may be able to understand you, most holy and righteous Father, and the love wherewith you have loved the world from the beginning, a love directed to all the people on earth, including our own mission.

We ask this of you, Father, for the sake of your Son Jesus Christ our Lord, in the unity of the Holy Spirit. Amen.'

This meditation marks a turning point in the course of the Exercises.

We started from the first principle and foundation of the story of David (which is the same for salvation history and for our own individual story), modelling this on the *First Principle and Foundation* of the *Exercises* of St Ignatius.

We then entered upon the *First Week*, reflecting on David's sin and repentance in the book of *Samuel* and *Psalm 51,* to become aware of the disorder existing within each of us.

We must now begin the contemplation of Christ, which opens the *Second Week* and opens with a very important meditation on *Christ, the Universal King*.

This meditation in St Ignatius's book serves as introduction to all the meditations on the gospel and is based on the consideration of the call of a temporal king, the better to understand the life of the Eternal King.

It is an invitation to know Jesus not only as a friend or as a master but as the One whom God has entrusted with power over the world, who asks us to share in his mission, in his life and in his sufferings, so that we may ultimately reign with him.

It is worth noting that St Ignatius always speaks of Christ, or even of Christ our Lord, but not of Jesus (cf *Second Week, nn. 91f*).

For temporal king we take David, and so must contemplate this figure's Christological content, his messianic role, the better to understand Jesus the Messiah.

We shall proceed by four stages:

— First we shall reflect on two fundamental Christological texts concerned with David: *2 Samuel 7* and *Psalm 89*.

— We shall then try to answer the question: in what manner does the New Testament view David's messianic role?

— At the third stage, we shall ask ourselves: what interest does David have for us?

— Lastly, we shall see how we ought to contemplate Jesus as the perfector of Old Testament faith.

2 Samuel 7 and Psalm 89

1) The passage in Samuel is the heart of David's entire story, the root of all the narratives about him. *1 Samuel 16–17* constitutes the primordial meditation — God loves David — the present chapter represents the central meditation — God makes a house for David — and explains why the Scriptures mention David so often.

The chapter falls neatly into three parts.

— The first (*2 Sam 7:1–3*) is very short and mentions David's proposal to build a temple. The prophet approves, and even encourages him: "Go, do all that is in your heart, for the Lord is with you".

— The second part (*vv. 4–17*) contains a surprise for us. The Lord contradicts Nathan, saying to him: "I have not dwelt in a house to this day . . .".

This saying contains an element of criticism of the Temple as residence of the Absolute, and the messianic burden of the text is temporal, not spatial.

Then the Lord reaffirms the first principle and foundation, his eternal love for David and also for Israel: "I took
you from the pasture, from following the sheep, that you
should be prince over my people Israel; and I have been
with you wherever you went, and have cut off all your
enemies from before you; and I will make for you a great
name, like the name of the great ones of the earth. And
I will appoint a place for my people Israel, and will plant
them, that they may dwell in their own place, and be disturbed no more; and violent men shall afflict them no more,
as formerly, from the time that I appointed judges over my
people Israel; and I will give you rest from all your enemies.
Moreover the Lord declares to you that the Lord will make
you a house" (*vv. 8–11*).

The revelation properly so-called occurs in *v. 11*: "The
Lord will make you a house". This is a solemn oracle, the
pivotal point, as it were, of the Old Testament; taken up
again by Isaiah, Jeremiah, Amos, Zechariah and some of
the Psalms.

It is not of course concerned with a house in the sense
of a dwelling but in the sense of posterity: "When your days
are fulfilled and you lie down with your fathers, I will raise
up your offspring after you, who shall come forth from your
body, and I will establish his kingdom" (*v. 12*).

In the days of the Judges, the form of government was
charismatic. To David, for the first time, it will be given
to have a sure descent.

V. 14 is very mysterious. We know that chapter 7 is not
ancient and represents the interpretative key to the entire
story of David. Probably *v. 14* is part of an addition and
refers to the king's successor: "I will be his father, and he
shall be my son".

The *Jerusalem Bible* observes that here we have an adop-
tion formula, as in *Psalm 2:7* and *110:1*, but, be that as
it may, this is the first expression of royal messianism: every
king of the Davidic dynasty will be an image (an imperfect
one as the end of the verse make plain, see also *Psalm
89:30–33*) of the ideal future king.

And the prophecy goes on: "When he commits iniquity,

I will chasten him with the rod of men, with the stripes of the sons of men; but I will not take my steadfast love from him, as I took it from Saul, whom I put away from before you. And your house and your kingdom shall be made sure for ever before me; your throne shall be established for ever" (*vv. 14b–16*). Note at once that these words will be re-echoed in the angelic salutation to the Virgin Mary.

— The third part of the chapter is David's response (*vv. 18–29*). A long and very beautiful prayer, full of tenderness, joy, refrains, repetitions, appropriate to someone aware of having been crowned with every kind of divine favour. I emphasise too the acute sense of physical relationship expressed by David; the assurance that his posterity will last is a window opening on eternity and therefore a marvellous promise. "Who am I, O Lord God, and what is my house, that thou hast brought me thus far? And yet this was a small thing in thy eyes, O Lord God; thou hast spoken also of thy servant's house for a great while to come, O Lord God! And what more can David say to thee? For thou knowest thy servant, O Lord God!" (*vv. 18–20*).

David constantly comes back to the *Lord God*, singing his praises, exalting his greatness, in a spirit of humility, compunction and trust: "Therefore thou art great, O Lord God, for there is none like thee, and there is no God besides thee, according to all that we have have heard with our ears . . ." (*v. 22f*).

At *v. 25* begins the prayer of confirmation. In the *Exercises*, St Ignatius recommends that, once the election has been made, he who has made it should with great diligence betake himself to prayer that the Lord may be pleased to receive and confirm it (cf *Second Week, n. 183*).

"Now, O Lord God, confirm for ever the word which thou hast spoken concerning thy servant and concerning his house, and do as thou hast spoken . . . And now, O Lord God, thou art God, and thy words are true, and thou hast promised this good thing to thy servant" (*vv. 25, 28*). When Jesus, in his prayer to the Father, says: "Thy word is truth" (*Jn 17:17*), we can read this as meaning not only truth in abstract but also his promises: your word is firm, you perform whatever you promise.

2) *Psalm 89* is the other Christological text, written more than five hundred years after the Davidic promise. It recapitulates the whole chapter in Samuel; the promise remains full of life despite the dark times through which the people of Israel are living. Now there is no king, no Temple, no priesthood; everything has disappeared, and the psalmist ponders the present situation in the light of God's oracle to David. This is therefore a great act of faith: "We don't know how, but certainly your promises are there".

The title is: *A poem by Ethan the native-born*. It begins with a prelude: "I will sing of thy steadfast love, O Lord, for ever; with my mouth I will proclaim thy faithfulness to all generations" (*vv. 1–2*).

The promises are next rehearsed: "I have made a covenant with my chosen one, / I have sworn to David my servant: / I will establish your descendants for ever, / and build your throne for all generations".

This is followed by a long hymn to God the creator (*vv. 5–18*). Textual critics opine that this is misplaced, but I believe it is put here on purpose to express the certainty that the God who made promises to David is that same God who created the heavens and who therefore cannot go back on his word.

At *v. 19* the messianic oracle is resumed on a more expansive scale. Thou who hast created the heavens and holdest the whole universe in hand,

> "of old didst speak in a vision
>   to thy faithful one, and say:
> 'I have set the crown upon one who is mighty,
>   I have exalted one chosen from the people.
> I have found David, my servant;
>   with my holy oil I have anointed him;
> so that my hand shall ever abide with him,
>   my arm also shall strengthen him. . .'
> He shall cry to me, 'Thou art my Father,
>   my God, and the Rock of my salvation. . .'
> My steadfast love I will keep for him for ever. . .

His line shall endure for ever,
   his throne as long as the sun before me.
Like the moon it shall be established for ever;
   it shall stand firm while the skies endure"
(cf vv. 19–37).

And at this point comes the question: why haven't we seen all these promises come true? how much longer is the present humiliation to go on?

"But now thou hast cast off and rejected,
   thou art full of wrath against thy anointed.
Thou hast renounced the covenant with thy servant;
   thou has defiled his crown in the dust.
Thou has breached all his walls;
   thou hast laid his strongholds in ruins.
All that pass by despoil him;
   he has become the scorn of his neighbours"
(vv. 38–41).

The trials the people are living through are dramatically described, and it is interesting to note that biblical faith is not afraid of arraigning God, of contending with him, like Job. To us, this way of taking the Lord to task may seem shocking, perhaps because we don't have as strong a faith as theirs, a faith amounting to total surrender to God and therefore entitled to arraign him. This is typical of the Israelite tradition.

The question receives no answer:

"How long, O Lord? Wilt thou hide thyself for ever?
   How long will thy wrath burn like fire?
Remember, O Lord, what the measure of life is,
   for what vanity thou hast created all the sons
     of men! . . .
Lord, where is thy steadfast love of old,
   which by thy faithfulness thou didst swear
     to David?
Remember, O Lord, how thy servant is scorned;
   how I bear in my bosom the insults of the peoples,

with which thy enemies taunt, O Lord,
with which they mock the footsteps of thy
anointed" (*vv. 38–52*).

The psalm ends, properly speaking, with this bleak view of history, yet there is a last word in conclusion: "Blessed be the Lord for ever! Amen! Amen!" This is in fact the coda, in the Hebrew collection, to the third book of the Psalter, but it is fine that it should figure here since it very well expresses the Hebrew spirit: Even if everything is going wrong, may God be blessed for ever!

Thus we have been able to see how the Davidic promise lives on in the depths of Israelite consciousness.

Messianic role of David in the New Testament

Does this promise — we may wonder — survive in the New Testament? The throne of David is no more, the kingdom of Israel has vanished, the people live under humiliating foreign occupation.

I already said at the outset that in the New Testament there are at least fifty-nine references to David.

Now I shall briefly mention a few of the texts explicitly referring to the Davidic promise.

— First of all *Luke 1:32–33*. The angel Gabriel says to Mary when speaking of the son she is to conceive: "He will be great and will be called the Son of the Most High; and the Lord God will give to him the throne of his father David, and he will reign over the house of Jacob for ever, and of his kingdom there will be no end". This is a formidable oracle for the history of Israel: Jesus is to fulfil the promise. And the angel's reference is precisely to the verses of *Psalm 89*.

— *Luke 1:68–69*. Zechariah promptly takes up the theme, although knowing nothing about the annunciation to Mary; in the small occurrences of his familiar world he perceives a sign that God is keeping the ancient promises. "Blessed be the Lord God of Israel, for he has visited and redeemed his people, and has raised up a horn of salvation

for us in the house of his servant David, as he spoke by
the mouth of his holy prophets from of old.''

God had said: "I shall make you a house" and now in
this house salvation has sprouted.

So this is what the faithful feel, such as Zechariah and
Mary.

— *Mark 10:47–48.* There is further evidence in the gospel
that the simple, poor folk too believe in the Davidic myth
and are quick to put their faith in anyone who looks most
likely to maintain it.

Mark relates that Jesus, making his way to Jerusalem,
arrives in Jericho where he encounters Bartimaeus, a blind
beggar, sitting by the roadside. When the blind man hears
it's Jesus of Nazareth, he begins shouting: "Jesus, son of
David, have mercy on me! . . . Son of David, have mercy
on me!''

— *Mark 12:35–36.* Jesus himself confirms his relationship to David, to go beyond it, not to deny it: "As Jesus
taught in the Temple, he said: 'How can the scribes say that
the Christ is the son of David? David himself, inspired by
the Holy Spirit, declared: The Lord said to my Lord, sit
at my right hand, till I put thy enemies under thy feet. David
himself calls him Lord; so how is he his son?' '' The people were very glad that he should claim the whole messianic
role of David for himself, also that he should claim it for
himself with a new, unforeseen dimension: he could be
David's son, yet greater than David at the same time. This
shows that in New Testament times there existed not only
among the Jews but among Christians too — for what we
have here is a fragment of Christian catechesis — a sense
of Jesus as Messiah and Davidic Messiah.

— *Mark 11:9–10.* "Those who went before and those
who followed cried out: 'Hosanna! Blessed is he who comes
in the name of the Lord! Blessed is the Kingdom of our
father David that is coming! Hosanna in the highest!' ''

The approaching kingdom of the ancestor David is seen
in Jesus, who appears with the characteristics of that un-
diminished hope.

— Lastly I offer a text from the primitive teaching of

the Church, to show how this interpretation continues.

Acts 13:22–23,32–34. Paul is speaking in Antioch and rehearsing the great deeds wrought by God for the sake of his people. He rehearses the period of the Judges, the prophet Samuel, King Saul, then says: "When he had removed him, he raised up David to be their king; of whom he testified and said, 'I have found in David the son of Jesse a man after my heart, who will do all my will'. Of this man's posterity God has brought to Israel a Saviour, Jesus, as he promised . . . And we bring you the good news that what God promised to the fathers, this he has fulfilled to us their children by raising up Jesus . . . And as for the fact that he raised him from the dead, no more to return to corruption, he spoke in this way: 'I will give you the holy and sure blessings of David' ''.

This last verse is not clear but seems to mean that the things promised to David are holy and cannot fail. They didn't exactly understand — Paul explains — how these things were to come about; we however know they have been fulfilled in the resurrection of Christ.

What interest do we have in the figure of David?

We may wonder what interest David has for us and why we should love him.

I have the impression he doesn't interest us very much. We take the view he was of concern to the Jews, who naturally rejoiced in the promise. However, from the moment we believe in Jesus as *Son of God*, the past has no more relevance. We've read the story, enjoyed it very much and that's the end of it; the concept of Messiah eludes us, and "Christ" as far as we are concerned is Jesus's other name. And thus we fail to grasp the historic sweep of the economy of salvation allowing us to realise that Jesus is the *Messianic* Son of God, head of a new human race. But it is useless to proclaim that he is the Son of God if we do not admit his presence and mission in history.

In another sense, I believe we have more messianism within us than we imagine. Possibly we are impregnated with so many messianisms that they prevent us distinguishing which is the true one. These are the ideological messianisms of progress, development, justice, freedom, democracy, all regarded as liberating forces.

Least of all can we renounce our vision of mankind on the march towards some high, definitive goal, a vision of human advance, not accidental, not pessimistic, not confrontational, but crowned with hope in a better and if possible settled future. This is the form historical messianism takes.

Anyhow, we have stripped the various messianisms from Jesus. We think of Jesus as God, and the things for which we fight — justice, human values — as things only concerning human beings.

Or, contrariwise, we have humanised Jesus, confounding him with a Messiah who liberates the poor, a political liberator.

David is important because he reminds us to keep getting our Christology back on a firm footing — since it is, in practice, always a little unsteady.

Then again, perhaps David is of little interest to us because Jesus *Christ* is of little interest to us; whereas being children of Abraham means sharing in the hope of Abraham and David, that hope being Jesus, head of a people, of a historic humanity, of a new people. We don't love David, because we don't love Jesus in his complete reality.

Davidic messianism is *personal history*: that is to say, the Messiah exists in a posterity and in a person. Jesus in himself sums up all the various messianisms, bearing them into the dimension of the divine: God so communicates himself to mankind as to raise up the perfect human being, Jesus, the Son of God, head of the human race, hope and centre of all history, synthesis of all genuine human aspirations. To understand what genuine human aspirations are however, we must begin with those that Jesus the Son of God represents in his earthly life.

Then our Christology will stop being ideological, or rationalistic, or humanistic, as is often the case, and be biblical Christology.

How to contemplate Jesus

The author of the *Letter to the Hebrews* helps us to understand Jesus as Messiah and what this means for his people and for mankind.

Having recalled the great fathers in faith from Abraham to Moses, from the Judges to David, he writes: "Therefore, since we are surrounded by so great a cloud of witnesses, let us also lay aside every weight, and sin which clings so closely, and let us run with perseverance the race that is set before us, looking to Jesus the pioneer and perfecter of our faith, who for the joy that was set before him endured the cross, despising the shame, and is seated at the right hand of the throne of God" (*12:1–2*).

This is a splendid summary of Christology and I suggest you meditate carefully on it, keeping the content of the preceding chapter 11 in mind.

The author speaks of a *cloud* of witnesses to assure us we are not alone in the race: an entire people is with us, helping us, acting as grand witnesses before Christ.

— On the journey of this people, we are first called "to lay aside every weight, and sin that clings so closely".

— Next, we ought "to run with perseverance the race". This is the race of which St Ignatius speaks in the *call of the king*: "Whoever desires to come with me must be contented with the food that I eat, with the drink and clothing that I have, etc. In like manner he must labour as I do during the day, and watch during the night . . ." *(Second Week, n. 93)*.

— Lastly, we ought "to fix our eyes on Jesus, the pioneer and perfecter of our faith". This refers back to chapter 11: "And all these, though well attested by their faith, did not receive what was promised, since God had foreseen something better for us, that apart from us they should not be made perfect" (*11:39–40*).

Jesus it is who sets the great march of the people of faith in motion, starting with Abraham, and brings it to its climax in his cross and resurrection.

To him it is therefore that the whole journey of faith

leads, and the ancients are the earliest witnesses to this.

What does Jesus do as the perfecter of Old Testament faith?

— He frees us from David's sin, from our wicked human nature; he frees us from social sin, injustice, slavery etc.

— He perfects the virtues of David, that intrepid witness to the faith.

— He teaches his people how to enter David's ordeals and overcome them as he overcame them.

— He attains and fulfils the hope glimpsed by David: peace, the Kingdom close to God.

We can now look ahead to the programme for the next meditations; these will aim at giving an explanation of the Christology summarised in the verses already quoted from the *Letter to the Hebrews*.

We have now seen how we get liberated from disorder, from David's sin, ever present within us.

From now on we shall be trying, with David's help, to contemplate the reality of Jesus, son of David, Universal King, Saviour of mankind.

So I suggest you reconsider the texts we have read together and ask yourselves: Do I love Jesus as the Christ?

'Help us, Lord, to grasp what you are for this people that is yours, and what you are and mean to be for your messianic people, that same people of the promises, given to you on the cross and at the resurrection.

Mary, daughter of David, daughter of Sion, grant that we may so achieve this way of seeing things as to integrate all biblical salvation history into our faith. Grant us to understand that the Old Testament is not an optional and preliminary book, but that it forms a part of our training in contemplating the fulness revealed in Jesus the Christ, Lord, Son of God.'

7

David's courage: Jesus's courage

'We pray you, God our Father, to let us know your Son Jesus, son of David, absolute mediator of salvation for the whole world, Lord of history, End of history. Grant us to know him as he knows us, to love him as he loves us, to contemplate him every day of our lives: grant us to share in the knowledge he has of you. We ask you this for the sake of the same Christ our Lord, through the Holy Spirit. Amen.'

We have already said that, following St Ignatius's suggestions in the *Second Week*, we intend to consider some examples from the life of the temporal king, the better to contemplate the life of the Eternal King, the Messiah, Christ Jesus. There are so many aspects of Jesus on which we can meditate, and St Ignatius writes that he is merely offering a few hints to teach us the *method* we should use, throughout the year, for contemplating Jesus, the Saviour of mankind and Revealer of the Father (cf *n. 162*).

I am going to suggest a few meditations for you by way of example, to make you more familiar with the interpretative technique of coming to know Christ by means of knowing David. As *method*, I choose the classic one of *lectio-meditatio-contemplatio*.

In the first and second parts of the reflection, we shall read and meditate on a passage about David (*lectio* and *meditatio*); in the third part, basing ourselves on the same text, we shall contemplate the life of Jesus (*contemplatio*). The purpose of all prayer is to worship Jesus, to taste his glory, to let oneself be impregnated with his divinity, shining forth in mankind.

Today's theme is courage: David's courage — Jesus's courage.

Lectio *of 1 Samuel 17:1–54*

David is a man of great courage and there are many passages bearing witness to this. Of them all, the one that stayed most firmly embedded in his people's hearts is his fight with Goliath the Philistine. Even people who don't read the Bible much know this famous story.

From the historical point of view, however, it is a bit tenuous, for the chapter belongs to a late tradition. The same book of Samuel attributes the victory over the Philistine to one of David's warriors: "And there was again war with the Philistines at Gob; and Elhanan the son of Jaareoregim the Bethlehemite, slew Goliath the Gittite, the shaft of whose spear was like a weaver's beam" (*2 Sam 21:19*).

Probably there was some confusion over dates: possibly David killed another Philistine just as terrible and famous, to whom the name Goliath was given at a later period.

Be that as it may, David's courage is a historical fact, and the fact that the Scriptures placed this long and splendid narrative in the *First Book of Samuel* shows that great symbolic importance was attached to it. The further we are from the sources, the nearer we are to the author's theological intention.

The Fathers of the Church commented on it at length and, interpreting it symbolically, used it as an instrument of catechesis: the struggle against the Adversary, bravery in confronting the Enemy of mankind, courage in temptation. And you know how often St Ignatius speaks of the Adversary and his wiles in fighting and plotting against mankind.

I leave it to you to read the whole chapter over slowly and confine myself to suggesting the three principal parts into which it can be divided, for making a good *lectio* exercise.

1) The first part *describes the situation.*

First, the site of the battlefield (*vv. 1–3*).

The literary skill of this passage ranks among the finest in the Bible. You are shown the lay-out of the camp; rather as in a film, you first get a view of the whole and then gradually home in on a specific scene. "Now the Philistines gathered their armies for battle; and they were gathered at Socoh, which belongs to Judah, and encamped between Socoh and Azekah, in Ephesdammin. And Saul and the men of Israel were gathered, and encamped in the valley of Elah, and drew up in line of battle against the Philistines. And the Philistines stood on the mountain on the one side, and Israel stood on the mountain on the other side, with a valley between them."

No particular individual is mentioned up till now.

In *vv. 4–7*, the *description of the champion* slowly takes shape. First of all, his name is given: Goliath. Then we hear about his height, then his helmet and very heavy coat of mail. On his legs he wears bronze greaves and the head of his spear weighs six hundred shekels of iron. Before him goes his shield-bearer.

In this minute description we actually seem to be seeing him and the feeling we experience is terror. We are dealing with a giant, a man of huge strength.

Vv. 8–11 tell of the *challenge*. Goliath launches his challenge, he begins shouting towards the Israelite ranks, and the words he shouts betray his deep contempt: "Why have you come out to draw up for battle. Am I not a Philistine, and are you not servants of Saul? Choose a man for yourselves and let him come down to me". *V. 11* is important because it underlines the effect of Goliath's words on the Israelites: "When Saul and all Israel heard these words of the Philistine, they were dismayed and greatly afraid".

2) The second part (*vv. 12–39*) tells of *David's arrival in the camp*. He too is described very gradually: a simple-hearted youth coming from Bethlehem (nothing is said about his having been anointed by Samuel, nothing about his divine election), who spends his time pasturing sheep. He has three elder brothers taking part in the war, and his father sends him to them with a measure of parched grain and ten loaves.

He also entrusts him with ten cheeses as a present for the commander of their thousand. The scene is informal, modest, in contrast to the events of the war and what has only just been said about Goliath's strength.

From *v. 23* onwards, the Philistine and his story become increasingly involved with this obliging lad, for David asks what is going on and thus assumes a part in the dramatic development of the narrative. Eliab gives his younger brother an angry answer and snubs him. Not in the least discouraged, David asks someone else and in the end decides to take the challenge up himself. He says to Saul: "Let no man's heart fail because of him; your servant will go and fight with this Philistine" (*v. 32*).

Note the contrast between the Israelites' fear and the lad's offer.

The king is unwilling to accept David's gesture, but the latter insists, telling how as a boy he had killed the lion and bear and assuring Saul that the Philistine would come to the same end as the animals which had attacked him, "seeing he has defied the armies of the living God" (*v. 36*).

V. 37 is particularly fine: David goes on to say: "The Lord who delivered me from the paw of the lion and from the paw of the bear, will deliver me from the hand of this Philistine". Then Saul said to David: "Go and the Lord be with you!"

The final two verses of this second part seem to put the lid on the whole thing. Having taken the young man seriously, the king puts a bronze helmet on the lad's head, and makes him put on a mail-coat. He then girds David with his own sword, putting it over the armour. At this point David exclaims: "I can't walk in all this, because I'm not used to it". And he takes it all off (cf *vv. 38–39*).

3) The third part is the account of *David in battle* (*vv. 40–54*).

First of all, David prepares with what little he has: his staff instead of a sword, five smooth stones which he chooses from the bed of the brook and puts in his shepherd's bag, his sling. Thus armed he advances on the Philistine.

Vv. 41–47 report a long verbal confrontation: "And the Philistine came on and drew near to David, with his shield-bearer in front of him. And when the Philistine looked,

and saw David, he disdained him; for he was but a youth,
ruddy and comely in appearance. And the Philistine said
to David. "Am I a dog, that you come to me with sticks?"
And the Philistine cursed David by his gods. The Philistine
said to David, "Come to me, and I will give your flesh to
the birds of the air and to the beasts of the field." Then
David said to the Philistine, "You come to me with a sword
and with a spear and with a javelin; but I come to you in
the name of the Lord of hosts, the God of the armies of
Israel, whom you have defied. This day the Lord will deliver
you into my hand, and I will strike you down, and cut off
your head; and I will give the dead bodies of the host of
the Philistines this day to the birds of the air and to the
wild beasts of the earth; that all the earth may know that
there is a God in Israel, and that all this assembly may know
that the Lord saves not with sword and spear; for the battle is the Lord's and he will give you into our hand."

These prolonged verbal encounters, with insults of every
kind, are characteristic of Old Testament man.

Between *v. 48* and *v. 51* the action is very swift and the
battle is described in half a dozen lines. David launches a
stone from his sling and, struck in the middle of his
forehead, Goliath falls. Seeing the giant die, the Philistines
take to their heels.

The conclusion comes in *vv. 52–54*. The men of Israel
and Judah recover their courage, pursue the enemy and
carry off a resounding victory. David takes Goliath's head
to Jerusalem.

Meditatio *on the text*

The *meditatio* consists in asking ourselves: What are the
key-ideas in the biblical passage? what sentiments are
emphasised? What messages in the story does the sacred
writer have for us?

Among the many themes I might have selected, I have
chosen two.

1) First, the description of the irrational fear seizing the
king and all Israel (*vv. 11, 24*).

If we give thought to the story as a whole, we realise this fear is out of all proportion. Goliath was very tall, a giant, but he couldn't have defeated a whole army.

David was to kill him instantly, with a little stone, probably because the Philistine wasn't a very agile mover. The Bible is clearly playing with symbols here: a man frightens great King Saul and his army, and yet a pebble kills him.

This is why I said the fear was unjustified and irrational, hypnotising the Israelite camp for no valid reason.

The Bible shows the absurdity of the fear for what it is, for Goliath has hardly collapsed before all Israel takes courage and conquers the foe. But they could have conquered them before, if they hadn't allowed themselves to be ensnared by irrationality.

Here I read the symbolic meaning of the story, which traditional spirituality applies to the Enemy of mankind, the Evil One who frightens us with trifles, who keeps us in subjection with empty fears, with terrors that in the ultimate analysis prove to be irrational.

So this is one of the messages and it conveys a very important spiritual experience, for we, as individuals and as a community, as the Church, are often hypnotised by fear. St Ignatius warns us that the Enemy, having no other power, relies heavily on this fear, resentment, sense of frustration.

At *n. 140* of the *Exercises*, he gives a description of the Adversary, imagining him as the chieftain of all the enemy on the plain of Babylon, seated on a huge throne of fire and smoke, in aspect horrible and fearful. The Adversary is seen as someone trying to impose his authority by means of fear, the sense of terror.

At *n. 325* (where we are given the Rules for the Discernment of Spirits), he then writes that the Adversary is not strong in any real strength of his own, but only owing to the fear he is able to inspire in our hearts. If a person begins to be afraid and lose courage in resisting temptation, there is no beast so fierce on the face of the earth as the Enemy of our human nature in prosecuting with intense malice his wicked designs. But Ignatius also says, if we resist the

temptations and act in a manner diametrically opposed to
what the Enemy suggests, then the victory is ours.

Goliath had bewitched the king and Israelite army with
fear. When the pebble struck him, the spell was broken and
all took heart once more.

It would be useful to examine ourselves, and examine the
reason for certain bad moods in Christian communities.
When people begin complaining about every thing and lay-
ing the blame on one another, anxiously seeking out the
causes why things are not going well, it means we have to
some extent fallen victim to the Adversary: he who injects
distrust and creates uneasiness.

Contrariwise, when a community manages to rejoice over
some small gift from God, it takes heart and confronts problems with greater clarity and objectivity.

There is no real justification for complaining, arguing,
forming factions, believing ourselves to be in the right. The
gaze of faith is sufficient for us to accept ourselves for what
we are and thank the Lord for the community he gives and
entrusts to us.

2) The second message I find in the narrative lies in
the comic contrast (the chapter is full of humorous touches)
between the *political prudence* of Saul and the *theological
courage* of little David.

Trying to act wisely, the king does his best to put David
off: "You are not able to go against this Philistine to fight
with him; for you are but a youth, and he has been a man
of war from his youth" (*v. 33*).

But his wisdom is confounded and the Bible shows how
God makes a mockery of the so-called political prudence
Saul seems to be exercising.

In contrast to political prudence, David represents
theological courage: "Your servant has killed both lions and
bears; and this uncircumcised Philistine shall be like one
of them, seeing he has defied the armies of the living God."
And David said, "The Lord who delivered me from the paw
of the lion and from the paw of the bear, will deliver me
from the hand of this Philistine" (*vv. 36–37*).

The two ways of acting are clearly opposed. David has his

reasons on which he bases his courage, which is hence neither stupid nor irrational. These reasons however do require the acceptance of a further risk: he has no assurance of being able to kill a warrior armed with helmet, sword and coat of mail, as he killed the bear and the lion. But calling to mind what God has already brought about through him, he realises that now He requires him to put his trust in Him and take the risk.

And he does this in a coherent manner, counting on what he has — staff, pebbles from the brook, sling — and the word of the Lord.

Saul, having first allowed himself to be seized with fear and then having tried to discourage David from the enterprise, gives in without grasping that the lad is putting his trust in God. He calculates everything from the human stand-point, dresses him up in the armour of a warrior and probably doesn't understand why David gets rid of it all and sets out with only his staff and sling.

This contrast between theological courage and political prudence constantly turns up in the Church's life too. Political prudence leads us always to be very sensitive to circumstances, to situations, to what other people may say, to what construction may be put on our words and actions.

In certain respects this is necessary, but wouldn't, as such, make much mileage for the Church, were it not for David plucking up his courage and going ahead.

We should often put the question to ourselves: Is what we are doing the fruit of courage, with spiritual and theological prudence, or is it in fact the fruit of a political prudence unwilling to take a risk?

The two positions aren't mutually contradictory to the point of being irreconcilable, but if the Church merely has political prudence for its inspiration, the Church will stand still, go on the defensive and that will be that. If David hadn't intervened, Saul's men would have stayed motionless for ever with the enemy forces confronting them. David it is who makes the breakthrough by ignoring all human considerations, scorning irrational fear, knowing the Lord can do all.

He doesn't take Saul's place, yet Saul should grasp the point if he means to escape from this immobility.

I'm sure, in your private meditations, you will find other messages too in this story, with its wealth of symbolic meanings.

Contemplatio *of Jesus's courage*

With the help of the reading and meditation, we must now contemplate Jesus and ask ourselves: When does he show courage, when does he confront the Adversary, when does he stand up to the Enemy?

I have chosen four occasions.

1) *Mark 1:12–13*. This is Jesus's first courageous act. David begins by overcoming Goliath, Jesus by overcoming temptations in his encounter with the Adversary.

Unlike the other synoptic writers, Mark describes the event very briefly. Jesus has had himself baptised in the Jordan by John the Baptist and has at that moment seen the Spirit descending on him: "The Spirit immediately drove him out into the wilderness. And he was in the wilderness forty days, tempted by Satan; and the angels ministered to him".

The Eternal King has thus confronted the One who inspires fear, the Enemy of mankind, who tempts him and would like to crush him. Jesus's public life begins with this struggle, to show that his messiahship entails conflict, that it is a messiahship of strife, that he, like David, embodies the role of fighter. When the Church forgets this, it finds its difficulties and problems bewildering; it worries over what to do next, without thinking first of all about confronting the Adversary. For the Church's life is lived in the daily drama of the struggle between good and evil, between light and darkness, between Christ and the Enemy of mankind.

2) *Mark 5:1–20*. Having stood up to the Enemy in person, Jesus stands up to him disguised in various situations. The example I chose for preference is his courage when faced with irrational, demoniacal forces inflicting suffering

through the Gerasene demoniac. This man inspires irrational fear in others and Jesus's struggle is not an easy one. He begins by saying: "Come out of the man, you unclean spirit" (*v. 8*), but the devil doesn't come out; the hurried conversation between them is then reported.

It is good to see Jesus fighting the irrational within us, all that part we can't manage to overcome: anxiety, nerves, fear, confusion. He struggles for us, carrying us towards order, harmony, peace. The narrative ends by saying that the people see the Gerasene sitting there, properly dressed and in his right mind, whereas before he kept injuring himself in attempting to end his own life.

By conquering the Enemy in the Gerasene, Jesus gives us the courage to resist the irrational forces in ourselves and others, as well as all those inexplicable disturbances that torment human nature, which, though striking us as thoroughly obscure, are expressions of the complexity of the human psyche. Jesus teaches us to treat these forces in such a way as to divert and direct them into harmless channels.

3) *Mark 4:37–41.* This is the story of the calming of the storm, of Jesus's courage in face of the unleashed, apparently uncontrollable forces of nature. Jesus conquers the human fear of being overpowered by natural forces, by death, and conquers it by calmness and by his ability to communicate this to the apostles and to nature itself. "He awoke and rebuked the wind, and said to the sea, 'Peace! Be still!' And the wind ceased and there was a great calm" (*v. 39*).

The apostles' fear was the physical fear of dying, so acute as to make them resentful towards Jesus. Jesus shows that his courage is born of faith.

Do we know how to conquer our fear of natural forces with the courage of faith: or the fear of dying, which certain natural disasters can produce?

4) *Mark 8:31–33.* I have chosen the fourth passage because it shows us Jesus facing up to the prospect of dying and dying soon. Clearly we might meditate on the agony in the Garden of Gethsemane but I preferred this text because it shows Jesus confronted with the prospect of

death quite early in his life, when he has scarcely begun his ministry: "And he began to teach them that the Son of man must suffer many things, and be rejected by the elders and the chief priests and the scribes, and be killed, and after three days rise again. And he said this plainly. And Peter took him, and began to rebuke him. But turning and seeing his disciples, he rebuked Peter, and said, 'Get behind me, Satan! For you are not on the side of God, but of men' ".

We contemplate Jesus talking about his death and rejecting as a Satanic act any attempt to divert him from it.

I therefore suggest you start with this last passage for your personal contemplation and then pass on to contemplate Jesus in the other ones.

'Jesus, however were you able to conquer the fear of death and talk of this death as something that had to be, that was the Father's will? However were you able to overcome your apostles' fears, when they were reluctant to accept your words? What was the key to your victory?'

We see that Jesus's courage isn't simply that of someone who says: God will help me. It's the courage of someone who faces up to everything and, having faced up to everything, then faces up to trivialities as well.

His is a courage very superior to that of David, who counts much on the Lord and only a little bit on himself.

Jesus has the strength to work miracles, he knows how to conquer demonic powers; but what is his strength against death?

Jesus, Son of the Father

His strength lies above all in being the Son self-surrendered to the Father, completely given to him. His sonship is the source of his ability to look death in the face, of his freedom of heart, of his courage.

On the divine plane, Jesus is at the centre, he is the Son who once and for all manifests and fulfils the Father's will.

'Jesus, teach us what it means to be sons and daughters, in you and with you. You are the Saviour because you are the Son. You are the true Christ because you teach us how to be children of God like you. This is the faith that conquers the world and overcomes all temptations.

Give us a deeper awareness, integrated into our personality, of the cry the Spirit constantly raises in our hearts: Father! — so that we may be enabled to calm our anxieties, fears, terrors and attitudes of excessive political prudence, and become free and supple, straightforward and meek.'

Theological courage comes from the spirit of sonship: knowing ourselves to be in the hands of God, the true Father of Jesus and, consequently, our Father; believing that Jesus makes us share in his attitudes as Son.

TO HIM WHO HAS WILL MORE BE GIVEN

(Homily for Thursday in the XVI week "per annum")

The gospel page we have just been hearing is one of those passages in the New Testament which cause us problems *(Mt 13:10–17)*.

Jesus has finished telling the parable of the sower and the disciples ask him why he addresses the crowd in parables. Jesus replies: "To you it has been given to know the secrets of the kingdom of heaven, but to them it has not been given. For to him who has will more be given, and he will have abundance; but from him who has not, even what he has will be taken away. This is why I speak to them in parables, because seeing they do not see, and hearing they do not hear, nor do they understand. With them indeed is fulfilled the prophecy of Isaiah which says:

> 'You shall indeed hear but never understand,
>   and you shall indeed see but never perceive.
> For this people's heart has grown dull,
>   and their ears are heavy of hearing,
>   and their eyes they have closed,
> lest they should perceive with their eyes,
>   and hear with their ears,
> and understand with their heart,
>   and turn for me to heal them.'

But blessed are your eyes, for they see, and your ears, for they hear. Truly, I say to you, many prophets and righteous men longed to see what you see, and did not see it, and to hear what you hear, and did not hear it."

1) People are bemused when they hear these words. We naturally explain them away as biblical rhetoric; the secondary causes get overlooked, the fact for instance that hardening of the heart is voluntary, guilty. And Isaiah is not alone in uttering this very forceful prophecy. Jesus himself uses similar language which has a very harsh ring to us.

Until the last century perhaps, this gospel passage

caused no problems: people were used to the idea that salvation was reserved for the few. The Fathers of the Church and many spiritual writers found no difficulty in dividing the human race into two categories: those who would be saved, and those who were not destined to eternal life.

Today however we can't admit this distinction any more, especially since Vatican II has taught us that salvation is available to all. We can't accept that there are people who aren't intended to understand, since we acknowledge the principle of universal equality.

The tenets of other religions, dialogue between religions, are important, insufficiently discussed themes.

In the Scriptures the idea of universal salvation makes only gradual progress, its starting point being the salvation of Israel, and we find universalist passages and particularist ones side by side.

When, however, we come on a particularist passage we are quite surprised and we then have to wrestle with the text as Jacob wrestled with the angel. We ought to turn to God and say: "Lord, you have placed us in this cultural situation in which we experience and suffer a difference of point of view from the ancients, from sundry passages in the New Testament, from certain expressions of the Fathers of the Church. Grant us the faith, light, discretion, passion, simplicity, courage to see your work in all the words of Holy Writ".

Hence above all it is needful to pray to Jesus, asking him to forgive us if we haven't always willingly accepted his gospel, and then we shall have to resign ourselves always to being a fraction divorced from his teachings.

Perhaps there is something in our mode of reasoning that needs to be put right, to be illuminated by the light of the Word of Jesus.

Certainly we mustn't avoid considering such passages in the New Testament. On the contrary, we are invited to approach them very humbly, slowly, never wearying of reading them and meditating on them.

2) In the Matthew text there is, in my opinion, a central saying which offers the key to resolving a great many

difficulties: "To him who has will more be given, and he will have abundance; but from him who has not, even what he has will be taken away" (*13:12*).

This isn't an isolated expression; it occurs, for instance, in the parable of the talents. From the servant who has buried his talent, it will be taken away and given to the one who already has ten, "for to everyone who has will more be given, and he will have abundance; but from him who has not, even what he has will be taken away" (*Mt 25:29*).

These words throw light on problems arising from either a personal or a pastoral context and, more generally, regarding inter-faith dialogue.

— From a personal context. "To him who has will more be given, and he will have abundance." First of all, God loves me; this absolute, fundamental truth is mine. I acknowledge my guilt, my sin, nonetheless God's love precedes my guilt. When I acknowledge that I'm a sinner, I receive forgiveness; joy, salvation, new life is given me in abundance. We cannot resolve our problems unless we start from the positive element within us, from faith in God's love.

Sometimes a whole series of problems builds up, one on top of another, and then, discouraged, we no longer know how to set about solving them, overcoming them. The right way of dealing with problems is to ask ourselves: What have we got already? Where's the firm ground on which to build?

The Christian life is a journey and we live it by leaving the place where we are. If I am nowhere, I can't set out; if however I am somewhere, however wild and inaccessible it may be, I have a useful point of reference.

God loves me. My certainty about this loving initiative of God's is the key to my existence: "To him who has will more be given".

— From a pastoral context. Faced with the more intricate type of situation, the question we ought to ask ourselves is this: Is there so much as the smallest point to start from? Is there so much as the smallest chink through which God's love can manifest itself in this situation?

Then we shall be given something more.

Returning to the parables: to the person who accepts what little of the enigma he or she can understand, more will be given. The parable is the offer of a tiny fragment of meaning, so that I open myself to this and to what goes beyond it.

This is Jesus's pastoral approach, always seeking to consolidate: "The Son of man came to save the lost" (*Lk 19:10*), to put good where there is none, so that, with this as starting point, one may progress.

— This gospel principle is also important where interfaith dialogue, and above all ecumenical dialogue, is concerned. We have always been nervous about this since it used to be thought that other religions were of the devil and that we were called to conquer them.

Naturally this dialogue, to which we are slowly becoming open, causes problems if it isn't rightly undertaken. Why evangelise if God may be found in all religions alike? Sometimes we come to lose our missionary, apostolic zeal, since there seems no point in taking so much trouble.

"To him who has will more be given, and he will have abundance", is the saying that helps me a lot in clarifying the problem. If we haven't understood, haven't tasted, the treasure of the Gospel, it's safer not to cultivate dialogue, not to travel the universalist road too lightly, or we shall lose the little that we have.

Anyone, on the other hand, who has come to know the mystery of Christ Jesus, King Eternal, Lord of history and mankind: anyone who has grasped what we are trying to do in the course of this Retreat, should have no fears whatever since he or she will henceforth be in a position to accord to every thing its proper value.

To anyone who, beginning with Old Testament salvation history, has penetrated the mystery of the Messiah, Son of God and Son of man, the synthesis of all human paths, all human aspirations and hopes: to that person will be given power to discern the qualities of value in other religions; will be given the ability to take part in dialogue humbly, unafraid and without reticence; will be given the joy of understanding the truth that is present in other religions; since he or she will be able to see all through the heart of Jesus, the pioneer and perfecter of our faith.

8

David's friendship: Jesus's friendship

'Almighty Father, we thank you for giving us everything in your Son and for teaching us to imitate him and in him find the truth about our whole human existence. We thank you for all the figures by means of whom you have prepared this mystery which is your Son, and we ask you so to open our hearts and minds that we may be able to read these figures and through them come to that sublimely deep reality which is Christ Jesus.

Lord Jesus, King of the Universe, centre of history, you loved us to the point of dying for us and you called us your friends.

Grant us to understand your heart; to understand the memorial of your death, of your friendship, which is the Eucharist.

Grant us to live in your friendship and to love one another to the point of dying for one another, following your example.

Father, hear our prayer for the sake of Jesus Christ our Lord who lives and reigns with you in the unity of the Holy Spirit for ever and ever. Amen.'

Always keeping the key-text from the *Letter to the Hebrews* in mind (*12:1–2*), we intend to ask ourselves today how Jesus perfects that friendship of which David offers so admirable an example. David is famous in history and literature for his loyalty to his friends and is sometimes even considered the symbol of friendship as such.

The Bible speaks at length of the bond between David and Jonathan, which emerges as the prototype of all friendship, even if sometimes the train of events related in the Scriptures inspires a degree of malice in the reader.

These stories have to be accepted in the simple spirit

of the Church Fathers, whose commentaries on them are magnificent.

We shall consider the friendship of David and Jonathan as a background to Jesus's friendship, which for us holds pride of place if we are to reach an understanding of God's plan.

First we shall make a *lectio* of a few texts about David's friendship; then a *lectio* of New Testament texts to see how Jesus brings friendship to perfection; finally I shall suggest five points for *meditatio*, leaving contemplation of the Eucharist to you, for the Eucharist is the pledge, the gift of friendship, the point on which all we're trying to say converges.

Lectio *on David's friendship*

1) *1 Samuel 17:57–18:4*. The narrative presents the birth of friendship between David and Jonathan as an unforeseen and total, unexpected and slightly inexplicable event.

David returns from killing the Philistine, and Abner brings him before Saul, who asks him: "Whose son are you, young man?" It would seem they are meeting for the first time. David answered, "I am the son of your servant Jesse the Bethlehemite." (*17:58*).

"When he had finished speaking to Saul, the soul of Jonathan was knit to the soul of David, and Jonathan loved him as his own soul" (*18:1*). The expression is a very strong one. In the following story, packed with cruelty, hate, revenge, suspicions, their friendship will be the golden thread holding all together by enriching it with true affection. "Then Jonathan made a covenant with David, because he loved him as his own soul. And Jonathan stripped himself of the robe that was upon him, and gave it to David, and his armour, and even his sword and his bow and his girdle" (*vv. 3–4*).

That was how it started.

2) *1 Samuel 19:1–7* is the testing of affection, the development of the preceding story. Jonathan loves David

and so at risk to himself he intercedes with his father, explaining to him that David is a loyal, faithful young man, full of respect for the king. Saul has informed his son Jonathan and all his courtiers that he means to kill David. Jonathan says to him: "Let not the king sin against his servant David; because he has not sinned against you, and because his deeds have been of good service to you; for he took his life in his hand and he slew the Philistine, and the Lord wrought a great victory for all Israel. You saw it, and rejoiced; why then will you sin against innocent blood by killing David without cause?" (*vv. 4–5*).

Jonathan does everything he can for his friend, and King Saul gives him a favourable hearing.

3) *1 Samuel 20* presents a second test of Jonathan's affection, when he defies his father's wrath by helping his friend to escape. The passage is very long, very fine and very vivid. I emphasise a few particularly important verses, that is to say, Jonathan's words to David, testifying to the theological, religious meaning of what is happening: " 'If I am still alive, show me the loyal love of the Lord, that I may not die; and do not cut off your loyalty from my house for ever. When the Lord cuts off every one of the enemies of David from the face of the earth, let not the name of Jonathan be cut off from the house of David. And may the Lord take vengeance on David's enemies.' And Jonathan made David swear again by his love for him; for he loved him as he loved his own soul" (*vv. 14–17*). Jonathan's trust is so strong, it goes beyond love and beyond the grave.

4) *1 Samuel 22:7–8* is the passage showing how the friendship between the two young men was a matter of criticism for the king: "Saul said to his servants who stood about him, 'Hear now, you Benjaminites; will the son of Jesse give every one of you fields and vineyards, will he make you all commanders of thousands and commanders of hundreds, that all of you have conspired against me? No one discloses to me when my son makes a league with the son of Jesse, none of you is sorry for me or discloses to me that my son has stirred up my servant against me, to lie in wait, as at this day.' "

In fact we know Jonathan has never plotted against his father and has been faithful all the time. On the other hand, he can't allow his friend to be killed and feels a strong loyalty to both of them.

5) *1 Samuel 23:15–18*. By a stratagem, Jonathan contrives to meet David one more time, secretly, out in the countryside. It is a climactic moment since it represents a proof of friendship bearing the risk of death for Jonathan. But he runs to his friend and encourages him in God's name (cf *v. 16*). Then he says: " 'Fear not; for the hand of Saul my father shall not find you. You shall be king over Israel, and I shall be next to you. Saul my father also knows this'. And the two of them made a covenant before the Lord. David remained at Horesh and Jonathan went home" (*vv. 17–18*).

At their first meeting, Jonathan gave David his clothes and his armour. The gesture was a significant one but perhaps also indicated that David needed them. Now in this new pact there is something more, a kind of prophecy by Jonathan who could descry God's plans beyond what appearances suggested.

6) *2 Samuel 1:25–27*. Friendship is not only experienced, but sung in very beautiful and touching tones in the elegy uttered by David over Jonathan who, with Saul, lost his life in battle:

> "How are the mighty fallen
>   in the midst of the battle!
>
> Jonathan lies slain upon thy high places.
>   I am distressed for you, my brother Jonathan;
> very pleasant have you been to me;
>   your love to me was wonderful,
>   passing the love of women.
>
> How are the mighty fallen,
>   and the weapons of war perished!"

What conclusions can we draw from these texts?
— We undoubtedly find ourselves faced with an

exceptional case of friendship in the Scriptures. A moving case since the two young men are both kings: Jonathan is the legal heir, David is the king elect, and we therefore have a competition in friendship between two remarkable people, of high relief. An extraordinary case, since either considered the other more important than himself. A case, indeed, that can have a somewhat ambiguous twist. The Bible however is so clearly opposed to all forms of homosexuality and homophily that it is absolutely impossible to imagine it intended to accept or emphasise any vicious element whatever in the relationship. We should therefore see it as an example of very exalted sensibility in a cruel and violent age.

— Secondly, in the narratives about Jonathan and David, I see the *central motive in David's story*. The love of God, who loved him and chose him, is so great that it even overflows on to his adversaries. Jonathan should have been David's enemy *par excellence* but instead is invested with God's love for him. By the light of an inspiration unique in the Scriptures, Jonathan has a prophetic intuition of the economy of salvation, of David's messiahship.

— Lastly there is an element which cannot be ignored. From these passages there shines the *beauty of a pact of friendship*, making the parties sensitive to each other, capable of sacrificing themselves for each other and of foreseeing each other's desires. This is something good in God's eyes too and for this reason is related in moving, beautiful words. The possibility of a personal pact that is neither political, nor economic, nor conjugal, the Bible deliberately emphasises as something genuine and good in itself.

Lectio *on Jesus's friendship*

Is Jesus, like David, susceptible to friendship? Is he sensitive to the beauty of the pact of friendship?

I have selected five kinds of text out of the many possible.

1) *Mark 10:17–22*. Jesus is preparing to go on his travels when he runs into a man, a rich one, who asks

him what he should do to obtain eternal life. He has always observed the commandments of Moses, and then "Jesus looking upon him loved him" (*v. 21*). This is an unexpected detail not occurring in the other synoptics, and reminiscent of the first meeting between Jonathan and David. Jesus has intuitively recognised and been moved by the depths of spiritual beauty in this man. Why the man didn't respond to Jesus's loving look is hard to grasp. Probably we are to infer that divine love claims no return.

John Paul II, in his *Letter to Young People throughout the World*, dated March 31, 1985, comments at length on this Marcan text, explaining how Jesus's gaze is the reflexion of that first gaze God directed at mankind, the reflexion of creative and sanctifying love.

Those who don't react in welcome to this gaze, who don't realise themselves to be loved, are luckless wretches, since ignorant of their true destiny.

2) *John 11:3,5*. This is another remarkable passage. The evangelist tells us a certain Lazarus is ill and his sisters Mary and Martha send word to Jesus: "Lord, he whom you love is ill" (*v. 3*).

This takes us by surprise since this is the first time Lazarus has ever been mentioned; we don't know who he was and even less why Jesus loved him or what the kind of relationship was between them.

Lazarus is, as it were, a faceless man, he has no features; in the gospel he appears to us with a cloth over his face.

What matters is simply Jesus loves him, Jesus is his friend. Not only him, but he "loved Martha and her sister" (*v. 5*). Jesus's friendship is expansive.

The parallel passage in *Luke (10:38–42)* is easier to understand: Jesus's informal visit to the house of Mary and Martha isn't an isolated occasion, but more probably habitual. His friendship with the three siblings was nourished by convivial moments: Jesus felt happy with them, he was an honoured guest and gladly took refuge in their house from time to time to relax. Not by accident therefore did Jesus hold his last dinner party, before the first great Holy Week, at Bethany.

So, Jesus was very much at home with these people and, even if the gospels don't say much about it, it is true — as someone has said — that Jesus had three "times" in his life: time for God, spent in night-long prayer; time for pastoral activity, for others, for the multitude; and time for friendship.

In John's account, by raising Lazarus from the dead, Jesus exposes himself to death, since the chief priests and Pharisees become convinced of the need to kill him.

His is a friendship faithful to the end.

3) A third group of texts refer to the Beloved Disciple.

— *John 19:26–27.* The foretelling of the treachery of Judas: "One of his disciples, whom Jesus loved, was lying close to the breast of Jesus; so Simon Peter beckoned to him and said, 'Tell us who it is of whom he speaks'. So lying thus, close to the breast of Jesus, he said to him, 'Lord, who is it?' Jesus answered, 'It is he to whom I shall give this morsel when I have dipped it.' "

The friendship between Jesus and John is totally trusting, with no secrets.

— *John 19:26–27.* The emphasis on the disciple whom *Jesus loved* is repeated at the decisive moment of the cross: "When Jesus saw his mother, and the disciple whom he loved standing near, he said to his mother, 'Woman, behold, your son!' Then he said to the disciple, 'Behold, your mother!' And from that hour the disciple took her to his own home."

The text has essentially a symbolic force, since John represents the Church receiving the graces of the cross. He has been admitted to a great intimacy, to the events of the Easter mystery, comprehending everything that Jesus does for the world. This is the sign that this friendship has not been left aside but now fully incorporated into the work of Christ.

Now turn to the event of the resurrection. Mary of Magdala goes to Jesus's tomb and finds that the stone has been taken away. "So she ran, and went to Simon Peter and the other disciple, the one whom Jesus loved, and said to them, 'They have taken the Lord out of the tomb, and we do not know where they have laid him.' Peter then came out with the other disciple, and they went toward the tomb. They both ran, but the other disciple outran Peter and reached the tomb first" (*Jn 20:2–4*). John however doesn't go into the sepulchre but waits for his companion to arrive. Peter comes up, goes in and "then the other disciple, who reached the tomb first, also went in, and he saw and believed" (*v. 8*).

— *John 21:7*. A few of the disciples are fishing on Lake Tiberias but catch no fish. At a given moment, Jesus appears on the shore without being recognised by them. He asks them for something to eat, invites them to let down the net once more, which is then filled with a colossal quantity of fish. "Then that disciple whom Jesus loved said to Peter, 'It is the Lord!' " What a great shout of faith!

— The close of the Fourth Gospel considers the future of this disciple. Having heard the Lord's word: "Follow me", "Peter turned and saw the disciple whom Jesus loved, who had lain close to his breast at the supper and had said, 'Lord, who is it that is going to betray you?' When Peter saw him, he said to Jesus, 'Lord, what about this man?' Jesus said to him, 'If it is my will that he remain until I come, what is that to you? Follow me!' The saying spread abroad among the brethren that this disciple was not to die; yet Jesus did not say to him that he was not to die, but, 'If it is my will that he remain until I come, what is that to you?' " (*Jn 21:20–24*).

All these texts deserve prolonged contemplation and we should ask the Lord to allow us to understand the mystery of his love for this disciple. It is hard to say why Jesus loved him more than the others. He was the earliest of the disciples; he sank his gaze into the depths of Christ's heart and grasped how Jesus the man loved mankind with the Son of God's heart. John was the one who lived that friendship from which the gospel of love was to be born.

4) *Luke 23:41–43*. I have chosen this passage because it is such a moving one. Jesus is on the cross and beside him have been crucified two evil-doers. One of them insults him. The other, though in his death-throes, has the guts to

rebuke him, reminding him they have been condemned to the same punishment: "But we indeed justly, for we are receiving the due reward of our deeds; but this man has done nothing wrong". He admires Jesus and turns to him in trust as to a friend: "Jesus, remember me when you come in your kingly power". Jesus replied: "Truly, I say to you, today you will be with me in Paradise". An amazing pact of friendship struck at the moment of death.

5) I draw your attention to two other texts which will help expand your horizons of reflection. In *John 13:34–35*, Jesus suggests himself as an example of friendship: "A new commandment I give to you, that you love one another; even as I have loved you, that you also love one another. By this all men will know that you are my disciples, if you have love for one another."

If we wonder whether this love is the love of friendship, we shall find the answer clearly given in *John 15:12–15*: "This is my commandment, that you love one another as I have loved you. Greater love has no man than this, that a man lay down his life for his friends. You are my friends if you do what I command you. No longer do I call you servants, for the servant does not know what his master is doing; but I have called you friends, for all that I have heard from my Father I have made known to you."

This is an explicit call to enter into the wealth of Jesus's friendship for his own, and to live it.

Points for the meditatio

What messages and lessons should we draw from the Old and New Testament texts we have been considering?

1) First of all, that *friendship is a divine gift*, freely given, a mystery; it cannot be forced, it cannot be rigidly programmed. It is a gift coming from above, and we should be disposed to receive it in a spirit of goodness, benevolence, courtesy and kindness to others.

2) Friendship is *beautiful* and gives savour to life, illuminates it, enriches relationships, changes people's characters. In this sense, it is one of the greatest of benefits.

3) Friendship is *faithfulness in trials even to death.* The story of Jonathan and David teaches us to be faithful at risk of our lives; John the favourite disciple takes his post under the cross, knowing it was a very dangerous place to be, knowing he could have been killed too.

Jesus says explicitly that friendship may mean giving up one's life. Hence it is a very rare and difficult gift. And not to be confused with comradeship.

4) Friendship *goes beyond death.* Jonathan asks David to be faithful to him even after death, and David was to be so by being exceptionally kind to his son (cf *2 Sam 9:1f*). Death does not put an end to friendship, as we see so gloriously in Jesus. For the Eucharist is the sign of Jesus's friendship in death and beyond death. Every time we celebrate the Eucharist, we celebrate the death of Jesus, who died for love, and we recall that dying for love conquers death itself. The Eucharist is the climatic moment in our contemplation of friendship; in it is faithfulness, perseverance, risk of life, eternal love.

So the *contemplatio* of all our meditation on friendship should be adoration of the Eucharist.

5) One last observation. *Can friendship be dangerous?* Experience tells us yes. All the finest things in life are two-sided, ambiguous.

We may exchange a false friendship for a true one, a constructive friendship for a destructive one, a friendship encouraging growth in the way of faith for a friendship that brings us to a halt or turns us back.

We need discernment here. The Bible furthermore shows various degrees of friendship, various types of relationship with others.

It seems useful to me to recall, for reflection, that a priest or a male or female religious ought not to have exclusive friendships. The friendship vouchsafed to us is Jesus's friendship, which we have chosen by consecrating our lives to him. Friendships are good, it is right to cultivate them, but we should live them as Jesus lived them, out in broad daylight, in the sunshine, sharing them with others. Friendships of the exclusive type eventually degenerate into ambiguity, then creating problems and suffering.

I recommend you to reflect on these points and I suggest you devote plenty of time to contemplation and adoration of the Eucharist, that memorial of what God has done for us; that burning bush in which is contained the mystery of the love of the Trinity, expressing itself in renewing, life-giving energy.

9

David's freedom: Jesus's freedom

'Lord Jesus Christ, our King, we are rather like the disciples at Emmaus who try to understand what you are saying while you expound the Scriptures to them. You know how important it is for us to understand what the ancient Scriptures prophesied about you. Open our eyes, Jesus, as you did for the disciples at Emmaus and for your apostles. Above all, inflame our hearts while you expound the Scriptures to us, so that we may recognise you in the breaking of the bread.

God our Father, we ask you this grace for the sake of this your Son Jesus Christ, in the unity of the Holy Spirit, in union of desire with the Virgin Mary and St Mary Magdalene.'

Wishing to know Jesus the Messiah better and to understand how his virtues and attitudes perfect the virtues and attitudes of the Old Testament, I now propose you a contemplation of David's freedom and Jesus's freedom. The theme is the *relationship between freedom and law.*

By way of introduction I shall begin with a passage from St Matthew's gospel; then we shall read a passage in the *First Book of Samuel*, quoted by Jesus; then we shall reconsider the passage in Matthew; from these readings I shall select a few short texts about the law, for meditation, to prepare us for contemplating Jesus's freedom. We are still within the framework of the second week of St Ignatius's *Exercises.*

Introduction

Matthew 12:1–8 is a text of great interest. One Sabbath morning Jesus is walking through the fields, his disciples are hungry, they begin plucking ears of wheat, the Pharisees

99

criticise them and Jesus defends them: "Have you not read
what David did, when he was hungry, and those who were
with him: how he entered the house of God and ate the bread
of the Presence, which it was not lawful for him to eat nor
for those who were with him, but only for the priests?"
(*vv. 3–4*).

These two verses refer us back to a passage in the *Book
of Samuel*.

Lectio *of 1 Samuel 21:2–7*

The passage occurs immediately after that longer chapter
describing the friendship between David and Jonathan.

Jonathan returns to the city and David sets out alone,
very frightened, not knowing what is going to happen to
him.

Reaching Nob, he encounters the priest Ahimelech, a
descendant of Eli. As a matter of interest, after the destruction of the shrine at Shiloh (cf *1 Sam 4*), the priests had
taken refuge on the eastern part of Mount Scopus, east of
Jerusalem.

On seeing David, the priest is seized with fear, probably
because he has already heard about the differences between
him and the king. He asks David: "Why are you alone,
and no one with you?" And David said, "The king has
charged me with a matter, and said to me, 'Let no one know
anything of the matter about which I send you, and with
which I have charged you.' I have made an appointment
with the young men for such and such a place." He thus
invents an excuse to get something to eat: "Now then, what
have you at hand? Give me five loaves of bread, or whatever
is here." David now has nothing; he is destitute and hungry;
he takes a first step towards making a new life for
himself. And the priest answered David, "I have no
common bread at hand, but there is holy bread; if only the
young men have kept themselves from women". And David
answered the priest, "Of a truth women have been kept from
us as always when I go on an expedition; the vessels of
the young men are holy, even when it is a common journey;

how much more today will their vessels be holy?''
His reply is rather a confused one but means they can eat
the bread because they have abstained from women.

So Ahimelech gives David the bread of the Presence. In
the structure of the *Book of Samuel* the purpose of this story
is merely to show that David starts out on his new life near
the sanctuary and that something consequently happens to
the sanctuary. Indeed, in the next chapter (*22:6f*), the tragic
outcome of the episode is told: Saul, having found out what
has happened, has Ahimelech and all the other priests of
Nob massacred.

These are not therefore explicit reflections on the law and
on a possible exception to the law.

Lectio *of Matthew 12:1–8*

Jesus however made use of this text in the *Book of Samuel*
to introduce a most important, fundamental theme, and the
passage in Matthew is the first of the pericopes about the
Sabbath.

Let me remind you of a few other ones:

— *Matthew 12:9–14*, the man with a withered hand
healed on the Sabbath day; *Luke 13:10–17*, the crippled
woman cured on the Sabbath; *Luke 14:1–6*, the dropsical
man healed on the Sabbath. A significant passage is *John
5:1–18*, the paralytic of Bethesda healed on the Sabbath and,
above all, *John 9*, the healing of the man born blind with
the long story that follows. The problem of the Sabbath
is a serious one, not trivial as it might seem to us, since it
involves one of God's commandments, found as early as
Genesis: God rested on the Sabbath and consecrated it
because on that day he ceased from all work (cf *Gen 2:2–3*).

Starting from the Decalogue, we find a series of minute
prescriptions designed precisely to safeguard the sacredness
of this day, still strictly observed by Jews even now:
everything is for the *simhat shabbat*, the joy of the
Sabbath. It is very beautiful for instance on the Friday
to see them making their preparations in an atmosphere
of enthusiasm, peace and festivity. For them, the Sabbath

is truly the day of rejoicing, dancing and prayer.

So the law of the Sabbath is a human tradition, based on a theological concept: human beings made in the image of God, human beings made not merely to work but to be happy, to live with God, to rest; human beings who, unlike the animals, can distinguish between one day and another.

The rhythmic alternation of work and rest is what gives order to life.

Jesus, as we shall see, connects the anxiety the Sabbath problem gave rise to in Pharisaic hearts with the individual's attitude towards the law, whether it be right or mistaken. It's a question of how to act where you have a positive law founded on a divine command and connected with the problem of knowing God.

So this is a difficult subject and prompts us to pray:

'Lord Jesus, grant that we may understand who you are and who your Father is; grant us to understand that we are dealing with a problem about knowing God. Grant that through knowing the Father, we may know you who are the Son and ourselves who are called, in you, to be God's children.'

— *Matthew 12:1–8*. The episode falls into three parts: in the first the facts are related; in the second we have the malicious comments of the Pharisees; in the third we have Jesus's ample and well argued response.

1. Jesus is passing through the fields on the Sabbath day with his disciples. The disciples, who are hungry, pluck ears of wheat and eat them (*v. 1*).

2. The Pharisees see them and wax indignant. Turning then on Jesus, they ask him why ever his disciples take the liberty of breaking the Sabbath (*v. 2*).

3. Jesus's answer lays down four very important principles:

The first is the *principle of commonsense:* "Have you not read what David did, when he was hungry, and those who were with him: how he entered the house of God and ate the bread of the Presence, which it was not lawful for him to eat nor for those who were with him, but only for the priests?" (*vv. 3–4*).

For your personal reading I invite you to take another look at a passage in *Exodus* (*25:23–30*) and at one in *Leviticus* (*24:5–9*).

Jesus cites the example of David to underline the fact that necessity prevails even on the Sabbath, that commonsense has its rights.

He knows David was loved, respected, considered a devout man as well as a great king: if he yielded to necessity, this means the law cannot not take account of need.

The second is the *theological principle*: "Or have you not read in the law how on the sabbath the priests in the temple profane the sabbath, and are guiltless?" (*v. 5*).

The Sabbath is divine, yet this is a relative, not an absolute, value; and what might seem to be a breach of the Sabbath, the Law says is not one: the religious activities for which the priests are responsible are not suspended.

The third is the *Christological principle*: "I tell you, something greater than the Temple is here" (*v. 6*). And one could add the final verse: "The Son of man is Lord of the Sabbath" (*v. 8*).

The fourth is the *ethical principle*: mercy, that is to say, prevails over sacrifice: "And if you had known what this means, 'I desire mercy, and not sacrifice,' you would not have condemned the guiltless. For the Son of man is lord of the sabbath" (*vv. 7–8*). God's economy is the norm for everything.

I think it might be useful if I said a bit more about the four principles, for these will help us reflect more deeply on Jesus's freedom before the Law.

(i) The *principle of commonsense*, easy to recognise, not so easy to practise. Faced with certain complications in the positive laws, we do not always manage to see where the commonsense solution lies. Jesus however mentions commonsense again in other similar cases: "Which of you, having a son or an ox that has fallen into a well, will not immediately pull him out on a Sabbath day" (*Lk 14:5*). One must not have such veneration for the law as to deny what natural commonsense demands. There is a priority of values instantly recognised by everyone, since the solution is dictated by natural commonsense.

(ii) The *theological principle* goes deeper. It explains *Genesis* and all tradition: the Sabbath is a very valuable thing, on it God himself rests, but saving one's fellow-being is always worthy of God. In such a contingency there can be no rest for us, since we are made in God's image. There is the case of the crippled woman healed on the Sabbath day, where the Lord retorted: "You hypocrites! Does not each of you on the sabbath untie his ox or his ass from the manger, and lead it away to water it? And ought not this woman, a daughter of Abraham whom Satan bound for eighteen years, be loosed from this bond on the sabbath day?" (*Lk 13:15–16*). And the evangelist notes that while Jesus was talking, his adversaries were abashed, while the crowd exulted over the great things he had done.

Jesus performs a work of liberating the conscience and the crowd is delighted: At last! This is what we think religion is all about, what we think God is all about; what he just said to us made our heart wince, but now we know instinctively this is the truth.

(iii) The Christological principle is even more developed: "I tell you, something greater than the Temple is here", where work is done on the Sabbath day.

The Law is subject to the definitive law of the divine dispensation instituted by Jesus, "Lord of the Sabbath", Lord of the whole divine economy.

Jesus is not only the humiliated man; he is the humiliated one exalted, the head of the messianic Kingdom, the true David receiving the Eternal Kingdom, he who institutes from this moment henceforth the economy of the Kingdom, the New Testament. Jesus is he who puts the new wine into new bottles, the new patch on the new garment.

In the new dispensation, the principle is Jesus, not the law, and he is the key to everything.

Understanding this is equivalent to beginning to understand the New Testament. In the Old, the sign was the Law given to Moses on Sinai; now the sign is Jesus, the eternal and definitive King, as St Ignatius says.

(iv) The ethical principle follows from the primacy of Jesus, Lord and Messiah. It is the principle governing all human attitudes, summed up in one simple saying: "I desire mercy, and not sacrifice". The reference is to the prophet *Hosea* (*6:6*), to emphasise the pregnancy of the term mercy, *hesed*, God's saving love poured abroad into human hearts by the Holy Spirit. And this is the supreme law.

"For I desire steadfast love and not sacrifice, the knowledge of God, rather than burnt offerings" (*Hos 6:6*).

Hosea links love with knowledge of God to show the need for a loving awareness, analogous to the love between husband and wife.

The theme returns in John: "This is eternal life, that they know thee the only true God, and Jesus Christ whom thou hast sent" (*Jn 17:3*).

And I should like you to note that Jesus and the prophet Hosea are both quoting a passage in *1 Samuel 15:22*, where God, through the mouth of Samuel, rejects Saul:

> "Has the Lord as great delight in burnt offerings
>   and sacrifices,
>   as in obeying the voice of the Lord?
> Behold, to obey is better than sacrifice.
>   and to hearken than the fat of rams."

Saul had disobeyed by keeping some booty for himself, under pretext of offering it to God. This text has made a long journey and, as we know, was used by St Ignatius in writing his famous *Letter on Obedience*.

The obedience better than sacrifice is not so much obedience to the rules as to the love of God, to listening to his Word, to getting to know him by knowing Jesus and taking him as the principle for every action. It is the primacy of *hesed*.

Jesus doesn't elaborate the argument; he confines himself to observing that the Pharisees' attitude to other people and the law is not right.

Even so, the principle is a formidable one requiring

reinterpretation of the entire Old Testament and the entire history of God and mankind.

Thus we come to the end of our *lectio* of the texts. St Ignatius writes that, above all, we should faithfully grasp the story, trying to envisage the situation clearly, the context, the associations. This is a suggestion you should always follow in your daily private meditation, for it is hard to enter into contemplation if we do not have as our starting point a serious and searching study of the biblical text.

Points for the meditatio

What should our attitude be to the Christian law? What does Jesus teach us as regards our freedom *under* the law, *through* and *before* the law?

I choose seven short theses in an attempt to reorganise what we have said up to this point.

1. The law of the New Testament is principally the Holy Spirit: "*Lex nova principaliter in Spiritu sancto consistit,*" as St Thomas affirms on the authority of the *Letter to the Romans (8:2f)*.

2. The Holy Spirit, as we know him in the New Testament dispensation, is the Spirit of Jesus the Son of God. This means the Holy Spirit creates a filial attitude in our hearts. His is an active, creative law; he puts our hearts into Jesus's heart, so that his sonship can live in us. The law, to express ourselves in ethical imagery, is being children in the Father's arms, being so for the past (our sins which have been forgiven), for the present and for the future.

In theological terms it means faith and hope: faith in today since the Father makes us his children now; hope as certainty that in the future nothing will be able to separate us from the love of Christ the Son of God.

That is the Christian law.

3. The Holy Spirit prompts us to love as Jesus loved. Jesus loved his own above all, and loved and loves all those whom God calls to be his children: "God shows his love for

us in that while we were yet sinners Christ died for us" (*Rom 5:8*).

The great and unique commandment for human relationships is charity, is to grow like God in love.

The life of Jesus is therefore our model for being God's children and for being people who love others.

This is the Holy Spirit, the law: to love as Jesus loved, to allow ourselves to be loved as he allowed himself to be loved by the Father.

It is rightly emphasised that Jesus is a *man for others*; nonetheless Jesus is the incarnate Son of God, is God for others, who unites us to himself by making us, by grace, like him in relationship with others. This is the Christian mystery.

4. The Christian life depends on this mystery: law, commandments, prayer, sacraments, liturgical year, pastoral work, customs, all have the purpose of making possible, or of re-establishing, the order of charity within the community. Everything is in the service of love.

5. What is Jesus's freedom in this context? It is the freedom of the Son who, feeling himself loved and spontaneously loving, respects the order of charity and everything connected with it.

In this respect, *Matthew 17:24–27* is illuminating: Jesus says that sons, by virtue of being sons, are exempt from paying the Temple tax, but should pay it nevertheless. We are talking here about an inner freedom which has no wish to overthrow the law, originally given to help the community respect the order of charity in daily life. Thus everything is polarised between Jesus's freedom as regards the Sabbath — and this denounces the loss of commonsense — and his respect for all those still outward laws the people observe, when these relate to the order of charity.

It is a most important principle for the Church: the freedom of the children should chime with that which concretely helps the community to live the primacy of charity (humility, good example, brotherly correction, communal prayer, forgiveness of offences: cf *Mt 18*).

6. We ought to respect everything that relates to the

origin of charity, with freedom of heart and spirit however, with the filial freedom appropriate to Jesus.

7. Finally, let us ask ourselves: what is the opposite of this attitude of freedom? It is twofold:

— either *anomia*, total lack of respect for the rules. One affirms that nothing but charity is needed and this becomes an excuse for doing whatever one pleases. From *anomia* comes arbitrariness, a kind of licence that wounds others in the name of charity;

— or, contrariwise, *rigidity*, lack of suppleness, of elasticity, in ecclesiastical or religious life; worship of the letter of the law, the pride bound up with that worship, hardheartedness, formalism, resentment.

Human nature travels, as it were, on the slopes of these two abysses. Jesus travels on the crest and invites us to travel with him, not thanks to our own strength or our own intelligence, but by the strength of the Holy Spirit, first and absolute principle of salvation history.

So let us begin our contemplation:

'Jesus, grant us to share in the freedom of your love, to contemplate your freedom, your existence as Son, your existence for others. Grant that from this contemplation we may receive the gift of the Holy Spirit to change our hearts and direct them into your freedom.'

PERSONAL EXPERIENCE OF THE RISEN CHRIST
(Homily for the Memorial of St Mary Magdalen)

The gospel text for the feast of St Mary Magdalene (*Jn 20:1, 11–18*) never ceases to fill us with wonder.

It announces the turning point of history, an event affecting the entire universe and its meaning. It is the grand opening of history towards the infinite, the manifestation of the love with which God created the world to reach this conclusion: *Jesus has risen.*

We shall never cease to marvel that the news of so solemn an event should be conveyed in a private, simple, informal conversation dealing with such human experiences as tears and weeping.

'How is it, Lord, that you reveal yourself in all your grandeur, yet do not overlook the littleness of our nature, the frailty of our psychological equipment?'

Similarly, starting from their sorrow, Jesus reveals himself to the disciples at Emmaus (*Lk 24:13f*) in a long conversation, in a survey of all ancient history and finally in the simplicity of a meal.

So God never ignores the petty details of daily life and today's gospel passage makes this very clear.

We may divide it into five phases.

1) First, Mary is mentioned as being near the tomb, especially in *v. 11* which is the true beginning of the pericope: "But Mary stood weeping outside the tomb".

Her weeping is noted four different times:

— weeping;
— as she wept she stooped to look into the tomb;
— why are you weeping? the angels ask her;
— why are you weeping? Jesus repeats to her.

The theme of tears occupies the entire first part of the narrative. The words of Isaiah spring to mind: "The Lord God will wipe away tears from all faces" (*25:8*), and of Revelation: "He will wipe away every tear from their eyes" (*21:4*).

2) The second phase comprises the conversation with

the angels. The angels are sitting on the grave-bench, one at the head and the other at the feet. They address the woman, saying: "Woman, why are you weeping?" "Because they have taken away my Lord," she replies, "and I do not know where they have laid him" (*v. 13*).

3) At this point Jesus appears and the conversation covers much the same ground: Why are you crying? Who are you looking for? — If you have taken him away, please tell me where you have taken him!

His mind full of Old Testament memories as he writes, the evangelist cannot fail to recall the words of the *Song of Solomon*: I searched for the beloved, I could not find him, I shall get up in the dark and wander through the city because I need to find him (cf *3:1f*). It is the great theme of the search for God, bringing us back once again to David's psalm: "O God, thou art my God, I seek thee" (*Ps 63*). We have already mentioned that some versions don't have "I search for you" but "I spend dawn with you". And Mary Magdalene goes early in the morning to the tomb.

The words of another song echo in the mind: "My tears have been my food day and night, while men say to me continually, 'Where is your God?' " (*Ps 42:3*).

All these references taken together indicate that Mary Magdalene, apparently being described as a private person with her own qualities of character, in fact symbolises the Old Testament search for God, represents mankind weeping because deprived of God and ceaselessly searching for him even if he can't be found.

Mary Magdalene is the type of all those men and women who, in our secularised society, seek God, yearn for him, thirst for him, long to see his face.

4) The search however is somewhat misdirected, is being conducted in human terms: it looks for God in the tomb, looks for Jesus where he is not to be found.

We have to admire the sincerity of the search, while together deploring the faulty basis for the means being employed. What a lot of people nowadays seek the Lord by means of human models of efficiency, success, power, easy satisfaction!

How impressive Jesus's behaviour is! He isn't put out
by the woman's mistake. He comes to correct our search-
ings, starting from what is good in them. He will behave
in the same way with the disciples at Emmaus, only with
them he will be a little sterner: "How slow you are to
believe!" With the woman he is more tender, probably
because she is better disposed than the two men. The
substance however does not change: the pilgrims of
Emmaus love Jesus and for this reason hope he'll be victorious; so, after the defeat of the cross, they are sad and
lament; motivated by love, Mary Magdalene seeks a dead
Christ. Each of them misses the mark, being very near to
God but not finding him.

The Exercises are a correctly directed search for God, conducted on a gospel basis.

Jesus comforts us by reaching out to the woman, asking
her a question that may well enlighten her: Is your search
a right one, is it appropriate?

Perhaps his insistence has already implanted a doubt in
her mind and, when Jesus utters her name, she is ready:
"Mary!" . . . "Rabboni!"

The resurrection of the incarnate Son of God is not
revealed by announcement of the event: I have risen! but
by the uttering of a person's name. The revelation is so personal, so existential, that it makes Mary Magdalene aware
of being known as she really is, in her totality and dignity
as a human being.

5)   Then comes the more theological announcement of
the ascent to the Father: Jesus makes the disciples sharers
in his filial condition, and they can then proclaim that he
is the Son and that they too are sons, that he ascends to
where they too will ascend.

All theology is no more than the elaboration of this
announcement.

The point of departure however is the private conversation, the uttering of our name by the Risen
One.

If St Augustine, one of the greatest experts on world
history and Church history, was able, in the *City of God*,

to trace the guidelines for understanding the unfolding of the ages, of civilisations, of the Church developing within the history of the world, this was because one day in Milan he was directly, personally, called by the Lord. Jean Guitton very truly observed that Augustine was able to write the *City of God* because he had already written the *Confessions*.

Once Augustine had begun to know himself as a person known by God, once he had understood the seasons of the soul and the process of his own conversion, he was able to transfer what he had intuitively perceived in his own personal story into a comprehension of world history itself.

This tells us that our personal life and the Church are not two separate entities, but that each flows into the other. We understand the Church in so much as we understand ourselves in our true life-story with Jesus.

We cannot understand ourselves unless we open ourselves to the Church and to all salvation history, to God's great teaching about the world; we cannot grasp this teaching if we haven't understood God's teaching in ourselves as individuals.

The teaching takes effect through pastoral activity: we cannot be shepherds unless we have experienced that God is our shepherd, that the ways of God are within us.

The meditations and extended periods of private prayer during the Exercises enlighten us, illuminate us, about the ways of God in our personal story and thus we become able in some degree to grasp the ways of God in the hearts of our brothers and sisters.

One final observation. The gospel passage underlines a new role for women. Mary Magdalene represents the human race, but she is a woman and as such she bears the news of the Resurrection. Similarly Mary of Nazareth utters her "So be it" as representative of humanity, yet she too is a woman. This opportunity to represent the human race and be the symbolic bearer of salvation, starting from a personal experience, is thus the typical privilege of womanhood:

to live in oneself that which brings salvation to the human race.

This is perhaps a mystery we haven't yet entirely plumbed and we ask Mary Magdalene on her liturgical feast to let us perceive more of God's design in this respect.

10

David's humility: Jesus's humility

St Ambrose begins his *De apologia prophetae David* with the following words: "I have decided to write an apology in defence of David. But this is not because he has any need of one, he having so many merits and virtues. Rather, because there are many people who read the story of what he did without any deep understanding of the spirit of the Scriptures or the unfathomable intentions of the One who dictates them" (*1:1*).

> *'We ask you, Lord, to let us read the story of David with the grace you bestowed on the apostles after the resurrection: the grace of penetrating the spirit of the Scriptures and of what happened to our forefathers, so that we may comprehend the spirit of Jesus and the reasons for his life and death.*
>
> *Grant us this grace, Father, for the sake of your Son Jesus Christ who lives and reigns with you and the Holy Spirit for ever and ever. Amen.'*

In the second week of the *Exercises*, St Ignatius speaks of three degrees of *humility*. The first consists in submitting and humbling myself so far as I can, in all things to obey the law of God; the second is not to bear more affection for riches than for poverty, for honour rather than dishonour, for a long life rather than a short life, if these are of equal use in the service of God and the salvation of my soul; the third degree and most perfect of all consists in willing and choosing, the better to imitate Christ, poverty rather than riches, contempt rather than honours, being esteemed as stupid for Christ's sake than to be accounted wise and prudent in this world (cf. *nn. 165–167*).

Intending, in the light of that passage in the *Letter to*

the Hebrews, to continue our reflections on behaviour traits that Jesus carries to perfection, I think a meditation on certain humble aspects of David's life would be useful.

Let us therefore make a *lectio* of a few narratives in the *Book of Samuel* and, after that, try to contrast the figure of David with that of Saul. At the end of the *lectio*, we shall consider how David's humility impinged on Israelite consciousness. Then we shall pass on to a *lectio* of gospel texts, which show us Jesus's humility. Finally, as a preliminary to the meditation, we shall see how the problem stands today, what Jesus's humility has to say to the pilgrim Church.

Lectio *on David's humility*

There are three episodes in the *Book of Samuel* which show us aspects of David's humility.

1) *1 Samuel 21:11–16.* Immediately after his meeting with Ahimelech at the shrine of Nob, David flees out of Saul's reach and arrives at the court of Achish, the king of Gath. On seeing him, the king's servants are alarmed, remembering what the Israelite women sang about David as they danced: "Saul has slain his thousands, and David his ten thousands". Naturally the fugitive hears what the king's servants are saying and he gets very frightened too. Craftily, he feigns madness: "He made marks on the doors of the gate, and let his spittle run down his beard. Then said Achish to his servants, 'Lo, you see the man is mad; why then have you brought him to me? Do I lack madmen, that you have brought this fellow to play the madman in my presence? Shall this fellow come into my house?' " (*vv. 14–16*). By these means David contrives to save himself.

This is a story about human prudence rather than about humility, and yet it shows that sometimes in life it is handy to pass for being a little mad, to get oneself out of worse difficulties. So St Ignatius while on a journey was captured by soldiers intent on doing him harm; he feigned madness and they let him go.

2) *2 Samuel 6:12–23* emphasises David's freedom as against human opinion. He isn't afraid what his wife

thinks of him. The narrative is rich in detail, indicating that Scripture attaches great importance to it.

Having journeyed hither and thither, the ark in which the Lord manifests his presence, returns to the Israelites. David calls all the people together and makes a great festival with songs and all kinds of musical instruments. Then "David went and brought up the ark of God from the house of Obededom to the city of David with rejoicing; and when those who bore the ark of the Lord had gone six paces, he sacrificed an ox and a fatling. And David danced before the Lord with all his might; and David was girded with a linen ephod. So David and all the house of Israel brought up the ark of the Lord with shouting, and with the sound of the horn.

As the ark of the Lord came into the city of David, Michal the daughter of Saul looked out of the window, and saw King David leaping and dancing before the Lord; and she despised him in her heart" (*vv. 13–16*). The ark is then put in position inside the tent the king has had erected for it. When the communion sacrifices and burnt offerings are over, David blesses the people, giving each individual a loaf of bread, a portion of dates and a raisin cake. "And David returned to bless his household. But Michal the daughter of Saul came out to meet David, and said, 'How the king of Israel honoured himself today, uncovering himself today before the eyes of his servants' maids, as one of the vulgar fellows shamelessly uncovers himself!' And David said to Michal, 'It was before the Lord, who chose me above your father, and above all his house, to appoint me as prince over Israel, the people of the Lord — and I will make merry before the Lord. I will make myself yet more contemptible than this, and I will be abased in your eyes; but by the maids of whom you have spoken, by them I shall be held in honour.' And Michal the daughter of Saul had no child to the day of her death" (*vv. 20–23*). We know moreover that the posterity is to be in the line of Solomon, son of Bathsheba, not of Michal to whom precedence would normally have been accorded.

The episode, a very fine one, shows us David's absolute

disregard for human judgement: God takes first place and, when honouring and glorifying him, we should take no notice of any critics.

This kind of freedom may well correspond to St Ignatius's first and second degrees of humility, a freedom, even in despite of threats, to follow the law of God.

To understand David's behaviour better, it is interesting to compare the passage with a strange incident in the life of his predecessor, King Saul (*1 Sam 19:18–24*). To escape from Saul's anger, David has taken refuge with Samuel. Having got to hear of this, Saul sends messengers to the prophet to arrest the young man; but these, on seeing the company of prophets prophesying, are possessed by the Spirit of God and fall into frenzy themselves. Obstinately, Saul sends other messengers and then others still: the same thing happens each time. He then decides to go in person, but when he reaches Ramah, "The Spirit of God came upon him, and as he went he prophesied, until he came to Naioth in Ramah. And he too stripped off his clothes, and he too prophesied before Samuel, and lay naked all that day and all that night. Hence it is said, 'Is Saul also among the prophets?' " (*vv. 23–24*).

On the one hand, the Bible emphasises the greatness of David who, to please his God, starts dancing without a thought of what people may say; on the other, the obstinacy of Saul who is eventually trapped in his own madness.

3) *2 Samuel 15:13ff; 16:1–14* is the most important episode of all, since in it we see David facing ruin and most painful humiliation. His son Absalom plots against his father and the conspiracy grows. David finds himself obliged to flee from Jerusalem, leaving his son a free hand. It is a stupendous story and deserves to be meditated on, word by word; three points emerge: the sacred character of the flight, David's calmness in this situation, his self-surrender to God's designs.

Thus the flight unfolds with great dignity like a procession or sacred drama: "The king went forth on foot, and all the people after him; and they halted at the last house" (*v. 16*). And all the country wept aloud as all the people

passed by, and the king crossed the brook Kidron, and all
the people passed on toward the wilderness (*v. 23*). Then
he sees Zadok coming with the Levites, who are carrying
the ark of the Lord; David sends him back into the city:
"If I find favour in the eyes of the Lord, he will bring me
back and let me see both it and his habitation; but if he
says, 'I have no pleasure in you', behold, here I am, let him
do to me what seems good to him." (*v. 26*). David has
achieved a very high spiritual stature. He doesn't struggle
against his son; he prefers to withdraw, accepting the
humiliation; and in his decision there is absolute self-
surrender to God's designs, a great affirmation of faith and
love.

Master of the situation to the end, he remains calm and
in absolute command. Ittai of Gath wants to follow him
with six hundred men but David begs him to turn back, since
it may be dangerous for him as a foreigner to throw in his
lot with the fugitives. Ittai is so impressed by the king's
magnanimity that he insists on staying and David then
allows him to join the cavalcade (*vv. 19–22*).

A salient moment emphasising David's faith occurs in
the subsequent chapter, when Shimei starts insulting and
cursing him. Abishai can't put up with this and says to the
king: "Why should this dead dog curse my lord the king?
Let me go over and take off his head." But the king said,
"What have I to do with you, you sons of Zeruiah? If he
is cursing because the Lord has said to him, 'Curse David,'
who then shall say, 'Why have you done so?' " And David
said to Abishai and to all his servants, "Behold, my own
son seeks my life; how much more now may this Ben-
jaminite! Let him alone, and let him curse; for the Lord
has bidden him. It may be that the Lord will look upon my
affliction, and that the Lord will repay me with good for
this cursing of me today" (*16:9–12*).

These pages are some of the finest in the Old Testament
and make one think of the songs in Isaiah (*chapters 52–53*).
We may contrast our own reactions when humiliated, when
we feel like immediately responding, reacting, without
knowing how to view humiliation in the light of God's

design. David doesn't allow himself to be overcome by the situation; he has faith in the God who loved him and still loves him; he doesn't lose his head. His behaviour in humiliation will succeed in reversing the situation.

What impression do we get of the figure of David from all these various narratives?

The first thing we must do is contrast him with the figure of Saul, since the Bible itself encourages us to do so. And I should like to quote the words of the Dominican Father J. D. Barthélemy in his book *God and His Image*: "In Saul's career, this is merely an event, a merely personal action: the dismembering of the oxen (*1 Sam 11:7*), for which the *mise-en-scène* of Samuel at Ramah and Mizpah has paved the way. Once, by this gesture, he has personally taken power, he persists in this power as he perceives it, and this obstinacy makes him go counter to God's designs".

The author then speaks of Saul's paranoia and I have made a point of looking up the definition in the dictionary: "Personality disorder, excessive pride, distrustfulness, excessive sensitiveness, duplicity of judgement, tendency to interpretations giving rise to delirium and aggressive reactions". It is a clinical description of the figure of Saul: a man obstinate in the notion of his own kingly grandeur who can't bear anyone else to exert any influence over the people.

He is the exact opposite of David. David is elastic, has no rigid concept of kingly power.

There was a moment when he let himself be snared by the temptation to salvage the king's dignity: this was the moment when he sinned. All the rest of his life however he shows great flexibility: he dances before the Lord, he accepts it when things go wrong, finds in every occasion a meaning, sees the good wherever it may be, seeks the ways of the Lord. A flexibility combined with humility, for he has no sense of self-importance or of playing an unyielding role in some grandiose design devised by himself: God it is who does everything in his life, God it is who gives him a house.

For this reason I think the notion, based on the figure of

David, took root in the Israelite mind that *true kingliness does not preclude humility*. With Saul, the idea still held good that kingliness was the equivalent of always winning, of always being right, of never being humiliated, of having a career of unwavering glory. With David, it is understood that kingliness can go along with humility, and this awareness we shall also find in the prophets, especially Zephaniah and Zechariah. Matthew the evangelist, describing Jesus's entry into Jerusalem, was to cite a verse from Zechariah: "Rejoice greatly, O daughter of Zion! Shout aloud, O daughter of Jerusalem! Lo, your king comes to you; triumphant and victorious is he, humble and riding on an ass" (*Zech 9:9*; cf *Mt 21:5*).

This is the mystery of this king. But humility is also proper to the people, not merely to the king: "Seek the Lord, all you humble of the land, who do his commands; seek righteousness, seek humility" (*Zeph 2:3*). "I will leave in the midst of you a people humble and lowly" (*Zeph 3:12*), the people of the Beatitudes, formed by following David in his humiliation.

Lectio *on Jesus's humility*

Not many gospel passages speak directly of Jesus's humility. More properly, it's the very atmosphere they exhale.

Nonetheless, there is one fundamental verse in which Jesus himself defines himself: "Take my yoke upon you, and learn from me; for I am gentle and lowly in heart" (*Mt 11:29*). Whereas, in John, Jesus is the way, the truth, the life, in the synoptics Jesus presents his life as a life of meekness and humility, but combined with kingliness even so. Indeed, a moment earlier, he said: "All things have been delivered to me by my Father" (*Mt 11:27*).

Such the humble kingliness, such the humble authority that shines forth in Jesus, with David as the model and yet in a different and much more perfect way.

St Ignatius conceived of Christ Jesus our Lord after this manner and so describes him when giving the programme of humility and poverty to his followers (cf *n. 146*).

We should re-read the gospels, asking ourselves: in what does Jesus's humility manifest itself?

I point you to two narratives which are somewhat apposite to what we've been saying about David, leaving you to find other ones for yourselves.

1) *Luke 4:16–30* is an episode I find very striking. In the discourse with which Jesus inaugurates his preaching mission, he presents himself free of the expectations of the crowd, unhypnotised by a desire for success, and he speaks without seeking applause.

In the synagogue the eyes of all are fixed on him (*v. 20*), they think he is going to say simply amazing things, but he for his part isn't concerned with telling the people what they want to hear.

And while for a minute or two some of them listen to him with interest, by the end failure is complete. Indeed, he makes them so indignant with him, they hustle him to the brow of the mountain to throw him off the cliff.

What does Jesus do? "Passing through the midst of them, he went away" (*v. 30*), goes down to Capernaum and, as though nothing has happened, resumes teaching on the Sabbath day.

His is an extraordinary freedom of heart. He doesn't alter his discourse to achieve a more favourable result; he simply goes to another city.

2) *Matthew 12:15–21*. This second passage is also significant as regards Jesus's behaviour. After the account of the plucked wheat ears, the evangelist records the healing of the man with a withered hand, effected on the Sabbath day. The Pharisees are outraged and plot to destroy Jesus, but "Jesus aware of this withdrew from there" (*v. 15*), like David leaving Jerusalem on account of Absalom's conspiracy.

Many people then follow him, Jesus cures them all, "and ordered them not to make him known" (*v. 16*).

Jesus could have exploited his power as a healer by inviting the people to go and tell the Pharisees what was happening; in this way the situation might have been turned in his favour. He doesn't do this, and his behaviour is so strange that the evangelist feels obliged to explain why he doesn't defend himself and why he refuses to gain any advantage from the good he is doing: "This was to fulfil what was spoken by the prophet Isaiah: 'Behold, my servant whom I have chosen, my beloved with whom my soul is well pleased.' " The words spoken about David come to mind, a man after God's own heart (cf *Acts 13:22*). "I will put my Spirit upon him, and he shall proclaim justice to the Gentiles. He will not wrangle or cry aloud, nor will any one hear his voice in the streets; he will not break a bruised reed or quench a smouldering wick, till he brings justice to victory; and in his name will the Gentiles hope" (*vv. 17–21*).

Isaiah's prophecy is mysterious: the Messiah will announce the true faith to the nations, not by using noisy means, but by gentleness; he will not break the bruised reed, he will not quench the smouldering wick.

The evangelist probably has the cross in mind, on which the true doctrine of God's love will be revealed. And in this cross, the symbol of humiliation, all nations will put their hope.

The text in Matthew is therefore very forceful and allows us to understand what Jesus was for his contemporaries.

It illuminates the simple, unpretentious, somewhat hidden life, availing itself of small means, that he led before the Passion.

The Universal King never divorces humility from kingliness and thus brings to perfection the way David behaved.

Introduction to the meditatio

How does the problem of humility present itself for the Church of today?

The people of God as such, and not only individual believers, is called to a humble, poor, inconspicuous life. On the other hand, the Church ought also to love the poor, the poorest, and try to help them. Social activity however requires costly means, requires us sometimes to sit at the table of the great ones of this earth in order to defend the rights of the poor, and all this prevents the Church from appearing to be truly poor and humble.

No indeed, it isn't easy to find a way out.

However I think it's very important to try and maintain some sort of balance at least: to love and choose humility because this was the way Jesus lived, and to love the poor, serving them and staying with them, with the means we have at our disposal, and constantly checking ourselves against the example set by Jesus.

Only by taking Jesus's life as our point of reference can we understand what we can do for others.

Let us ask the Virgin Mary to make us always love the way of simplicity and humility, so that we too can love the poor, the humiliated, the persecuted of this world with all the strength we have and with all the love we bear for Jesus.

11

David's ordeals: Jesus's ordeals

"Remember, O Lord, in David's favour, all the hardships he endured" (*Ps 132:1*). This can also be translated: "Remember David, Lord, and all his *ordeals*". By means of these ordeals, God will prepare a lamp for his Messiah; he will clothe his enemies with shame and make his crown shed its lustre on him (cf *vv. 17–18*).

'Help us, God our Father, to understand David's ordeals, to enter into his sufferings and problems. Help us to understand his struggle against his enemies and that of the enemies against him, so that we by this may enter into the sufferings and ordeals of your Son Jesus Christ, the Universal King. In him it pleased you to cleanse our human nature and so you alone can give us grace to contemplate the cross. We ask you this, Father, for the sake of Christ our Lord.'

The purpose of this meditation is to serve as bridge between the second and third week of St Ignatius's *Exercises*, in the desire of letting ourselves be conquered by Christ (cf *Philemon 3:12*) so that we may be ever more closely united to him.

We shall begin with a *lectio* on David's ordeals, next we shall try to comprehend the message; thence to the *lectio* and message of Jesus's ordeals.

Lectio *on David's ordeals*

David's ordeals occupy a large part of the *Books of Samuel*. As you glance through the Bible, you will immediately realise the very titles of the stories indicate that this is so. I think it will be helpful to divide the ordeals into personal, political and family ones.

1) *Personal ordeals.* Unlike Saul who is portrayed as prey to fearful existential anxieties, the Scriptures do not speak of David as a man tormented by strong temptations, by fear, or by doubt. On the contrary, he is an optimist, always looking for the way out, who puts his trust in God with great hope.

— All the same, there are the exceptions in his life; I confine myself to reminding you of the passage in *1 Samuel 30:3–6*: the Amalekites make a raid on David's people at Ziklag in the Negeb when he himself is somewhere else. When he comes back he finds the town in flames and is distracted because of not having foreseen the disaster: "Then David and the people who were with him raised their voices and wept, until they had no more strength to weep. David's two wives also had been taken captive, Ahinoam of Jezreel, and Abigail the widow of Nabal of Carmel. And *David was greatly distressed*; for the people spoke of stoning him, because all the people were bitter in soul, each for his sons and daughters. But David strengthened himself in the Lord his God" (*vv. 4–6*).

This is a very significant passage. David's agony of mind is not simple grief; it is a sort of desperation, since the people want to stone him. Moses too had more than once felt what a weight it was to be responsible for people who bore a grudge and rebelled against him.

David however quickly takes a grip on himself, puts his trust in God, consulting him and asking what to do (*v. 8*).

— But for a deeper knowledge about David's personal ordeals, we must have recourse to the Psalms, to *Psalm 42* for instance, which is not directly attributed to him but has much in common with *Psalm 63*: "My tears have been my food day and night, while men say to me continually, 'Where is your God?' . . . Why are you cast down, O my soul, and why are you disquieted within me? . . . My soul is cast down within me, therefore I remember thee . . . I say to my God, my rock: 'Why hast thou forgotten me?' . . . My adversaries taunt me, while they say to me continually, 'Where is your God?' . . . Why are you cast down, O my soul, and why are you disquieted within me?"

David experiences two feelings in these ordeals. First, *loneliness*: he feels himself to be deserted, misunderstood. And since any one of us can have a similar experience, I should like to emphasise that the Psalms can give us a great deal of comfort, since they tell of loneliness and help us to overcome it. It is told of St Charles Borromeo, a very strong, brave, even hard man, that when he was out riding one day with his cousin Federigo, a man considerably younger than himself, the latter suddenly asked him: "What do you do in moments of distress?" The saint took a little Psalter from his pocket and replied: "I read the psalms".

David furthermore feels *he has enemies*, people who wish him ill. To young people perhaps it may seem strange that the Psalms should speak so much about "enemies surrounding me", mocking me, despising me, but with the passing of time we come to realise that in fact there are people who, because of our mistakes or those of others, are against us.

Again, the psalms have something appropriate to say: "Vindicate me, O God, and defend my cause against an ungodly people; from deceitful and unjust men deliver me" (*Ps 43:1*). Not a judgement to be given against others, but a prayer that the Lord will help us when we find ourselves in difficulty and do not know the reason for the hostile behaviour of those around us.

2) The *political and social ordeals* of David are described at length and start at the very outset.

— *1 Samuel 18:7*, according to Père J. D. Barthélemy, is the key-verse to all the ordeals that follow: "The women sang to one another as they made merry: 'Saul has slain his thousands, and David his ten thousands' ". This is the beginning of troubles, for Saul is furious when he hears this song.

Perhaps Scripture is trying to tell us to mistrust praise, since this can always give rise to jealousy and incomprehension. You need only think of the intrigues over the succession, once Saul was dead.

— David waits, secure in God's promise; he does nothing towards becoming king, does not kill Saul, defends himself as well as he can, even, to survive, becoming a vassal of the Philistines. Thus he is right before God, thus free to enter easily into relations with the Philistines, the enemies of Israel, while still remaining faithful to his own people. Saul persisted in seeing the way as he himself imagined it to be; David, in contrast, doesn't consider the problem of the future but surrenders himself into the Lord's hands. That is what's meant by David's gift of wisdom, freedom, suppleness.

Chapters 28 & 29 of the *First Book of Samuel* are significant in this respect. The Philistines muster their army to fight the people of God, and David, who up to this moment has had no problems, does not know how to act. Achish orders David and his men to take the field with him. David replies: "Very well, you shall know what your servant can do" (*28:2*). He tries to get out of doing this, putting his trust in God and hoping that future events will dispense him from fighting against Israel. But Achish says to him, "Very well, I will make you my bodyguard for life" (*v. 2*).

We know, from the continuation of the story, that Providence intervenes: the Philistines concentrate all their men at Aphek, then ask Achish for information about David: "Is not this David, the servant of Saul, king of Israel, who has been with me now for days and years, and since he deserted to me I have found no fault in him to this day?" But the commanders of the Philistines were angry with him; and the commanders of the Philistines said to him, "Send the man back, that he may return to the place to which you have assigned him; he shall not go down with us to battle, lest in the battle he become an adversary to us" (*29:3–4*). Achish then summons David and requests him to withdraw, rather than upset the Philistine leaders. In this unexpected way, the solution comes. The passage is loaded with irony, for David complains to Achish about being treated like this: "But what have I done? What have you found in your servant from the day I entered your service until now, that I may not go and fight against the enemies of my lord the king?" And Achish made answer to David, "I know that you are as blameless in my sight as an angel of God;

nevertheless the commanders of the Philistines have said, 'He shall not go up with us to the battle' " (*vv. 8–9*). The Philistines do battle with Israel and the Israelites flee up Mount Gilboah where Saul is slain. David for his part hasn't raised a finger against his people. And thus the Bible emphasises that, even when we live in the midst of enemies, we should remain consistent and loyal to God and to our own people.

3) David's *family ordeals* are very severe, especially towards the end of his life. His own family, whom he loves so much, falls victim to notions of royal prestige, to lust for power, fraternal strife, jealousy. And David doesn't succeed in keeping it united.

This then is the greatest tragedy for his passionate, magnanimous heart and reaches its climax in the death of his son Absalom. David has done everything he can to avoid fighting him and to overlook his intrigues. But when he receives the news that Absalom has been killed, he bursts into tears: "O my son Absalom, my son, my son Absalom! Would I had died instead of you, O Absalom, my son, my son!" (*2 Sam 18:33; 19:1f*). The king's cry is one of the peaks of the whole Old Testament, for it shows how the heart takes precedence over all. Not kingly glory, not affairs of state, can matter as much as love.

In this lament of David's, it's easy for us to read a prophecy of the heart of Jesus. To each of us he says: My child, you have injured yourself by your sin but I am willing to die instead of you!

Meditatio *on David's ordeals*

What is the message, how is it interpreted in Israelite history?

Let us link up with our reflections of yesterday: the office of king, the office of Messiah, is also exercised in ordeal and suffering. David endured his ordeals with faith, with love, with loyalty, with trust in God.

Messianism has its lights, its glories, its splendours and it also has its shadows and gloom. The kingly office is often exercised in suffering, especially in suffering for others, for the people; David suffers as king and as representative symbolising the whole nation.

Better than any other prophet, Isaiah helps us to understand Jesus's kingly behaviour in the light of this Davidic tradition: "A man of sorrows and acquainted with grief . . . he was despised and we esteemed him not". But can this man be the Saviour? The answer comes further on:

> "Surely he has borne our griefs
>   and carried our sorrows;
> yet we esteemed him stricken,
>   smitten by God, and afflicted.
> But he was wounded for our transgressions,
>   he was bruised for our iniquities;
> upon him was the chastisement that made us whole,
>   and with his stripes we are healed" (*Is 53:3–5*).

These mysterious words were written by the prophet while reflecting on the great sufferings of the Chosen People, possibly on the prophet's own sufferings, but certainly also with David in mind:

> "Who has believed what we have heard?
>   And to whom has the arm of the Lord been
>   revealed?
> For he grew up before him like a young plant,
>   and like a root out of dry ground" (*Is 53:1–2*).

The young plant was the one which was to sprout from the stock of Jesse and grow out of his roots; on him would rest the Spirit of the Lord (cf *Is 11:1–2*).

He went through suffering and ordeal for love of his people.

The point absorbed into Israelite awareness is that the king designated by God will have to pass through ordeal, that suffering forms part of the story of any true king who has his people's welfare at heart.

In Isaiah's meditations we can also find an answer to the question on which *Psalm 89* comes to an end.

"Lord, where is thy steadfast love of old,
 which by thy faithfulness thou didst swear
  to David?
Remember, O Lord, how thy servant is scorned;
 how I bear in my bosom the insults of the peoples,
with which thy enemies taunt, O Lord,
 with which they mock the footsteps of thy
  anointed" (*vv. 49–51*).

Nothing odd about this, says Isaiah: he is suffering for his people's sake; David, the king beloved and chosen by God, has been through this already.

Lectio *on Jesus's ordeals*

St Ignatius, in the third week, would have us ask for the grace of *being with Jesus*, sharing too in all his ordeals. Let us ask for this, so that we may arrive at true knowledge of Christ the Universal King, the son of David.

Let's repeat the lay-out of the previous reflexion.

1) The *personal ordeals* of Jesus. As with David, we don't have many texts to allow us to investigate Jesus's inner experiences.

I mention one or two passages that seem to me worth consideration.

— *Mark 8:12*. The Pharisees ask for a sign from heaven. "He sighed deeply in spirit and said, 'Why does this generation seek a sign?' "

The anguish and uneasiness emphasised by the evangelist recurs in

— *Mark 9:19*. An epileptic demoniac whom the disciples haven't been able to cure is brought to Jesus, who exclaims: "O faithless generation! How long am I to be with you? How long am I to bear with you?" It's strange, hearing Jesus say: I've had enough of you.

— The most disturbing passage however is *Mark 14:33–34*. After instituting the Eucharist, Jesus leaves for the Mount of Olives; having reached a place called Gethsemane, he takes Peter, James and John with him.

Then "he began to be greatly distressed and troubled. And he said to them, 'My soul is very sorrowful, even unto death; remain here and pray' ".

Fear, anguish, grief. Jesus has now entered that terrible moment in his career when he would like to give the whole thing up; he has asked us not to leave him on his own but to shoulder our small share in his ordeal.

— Many of the psalms are quoted in the New Testament to depict Jesus's personal anguish. For instance:

> "I am poured out like water,
>   and all my bones are out of joint;
> my heart is like wax,
>   it is melted within my breast;
> my strength is dried up like a potsherd,
>   and my tongue cleaves to my jaws;
>   thou dost lay me in the dust of death."
>
> *(Ps 22:14–15)*

We are dealing with an inner and outward distress that seizes on the heart, making it difficult to speak or think.

I leave it of course to you to meditate privately on the complete text of the agony in Gethsemane, so as to understand to what lengths Jesus was prepared to go, to demonstrate his love to us.

2) *Political and social ordeals.* Jesus had all the authorities against him. None of them understood him properly and from the outset the political and religious leaders felt uneasy to say the least in their encounters with him.

— Significant of this is the interpretation put on *Psalm 2* in the *Acts of the Apostles*: "Lord, who didst make the heaven and the earth and the sea and everything in them, who by the mouth of our father David, thy servant, didst say by the Holy Spirit,

> 'Why did the Gentiles rage,
>   and the peoples imagine vain things?
> The kings of the earth set themselves in array,
>   and the rulers were gathered together,

against the Lord and against his
    Anointed'—
for truly in this city there were gathered together against
thy holy servant Jesus, whom thou didst anoint, both Herod
and Pontius Pilate, with the Gentiles and the peoples of
Israel, to do whatever thy hand and thy plan had predestined
to take place'' (*Acts 4:24–28*).

Jesus has nothing against authority, he never exploits his
popularity to set the multitude against it, he does not disobey
the laws. The ill-will the leaders bear him, which will lead
them to decide to crucify him, is totally unaccountable and
has to be seen in the light of the divine plan of salvation.

— Jesus does not let himself be stopped by the
authorities. We read for instance that when, at the end of
his discourse in the synagogue, he is hustled out of the town
and up the hill to be thrown over the cliff, "passing through
the midst of them, he went away" (*Lk 4:30*).

The evangelist intends a symbolic description of Jesus's
behaviour in this world: *he passes through the midst,*
without going against the authorities, without resisting either
actively or passively.

He goes right ahead, indifferent to the various forms
of opposition and difficulty. And when the various forms
of opposition coalesce to sentence him to death, he
accepts.

We see this attitude of Jesus's in connection with one particular authority, Herod: "Some Pharisees came, and said
to him, 'Get away from here, for Herod wants to kill you.'
And he said to them, 'Go and tell that fox, "Behold, I cast
out demons and perform cures today and tomorrow, and
the third day I finish my course. Nevertheless I must go on
my way today and tomorrow and the day following; for
it cannot be that a prophet should perish away from
Jerusalem" ' '' (*Lk 13:31–33*).

David had the political ability of entering into relations
with his enemies and from this getting whatever might prove
useful for him or his people. Jesus perfects David's attitude;
he deals with those who are hostile to him, not by giving
in but by keeping on going towards his goal.

3) *Family ordeals*. Jesus's brothers and relatives do not understand him and give him neither comfort nor support. We read for instance in *Mark 3:20–21* that, hearing it said that because of the enormous crowd thronging to see him he didn't even have time to eat, "his own" set out to take charge of him, convinced that he was out of his mind.

In *John 7:2*, Jesus is travelling round Galilee as the Jewish feast of Tabernacles draws near. "So his brothers said to him, 'Leave here and go to Judea, that your disciples may see the works you are doing. For no man works in secret if he seeks to be known openly. If you do these things, show yourself to the world' ". His brothers do not understand him, or rather they claim for him a kingship of success, honour, prestige, on the lines of the kingship of Saul.

— But there is a ruder ordeal for Jesus and this is due to the lack of understanding on the part of his disciples, on the part of those whom he has called "brother, sister and mother" (cf *Mk 3:35*) and to whom he is bound by an absolute, convenantal pact.

Mark 8:17f: "Why do you discuss the fact that you have no bread? Do you not yet perceive or understand? Are your hearts hardened? Having eyes do you not see, and having ears do you not hear? And do you not remember, when I broke the five loaves for the five thousand . . ." We ought to reflect lengthily on this passage, underlining as it does the difficulty Jesus had in getting his disciples to understand him.

Mark 14:18f: this describes the failure of friendship, as experienced by Jesus. First the traitor Judas, then the flight of the other apostles and Peter's denial. His dearest, best beloved friends have left him on his own, have done nothing to comfort him or alleviate his ordeal.

So we may say Jesus experienced two profound sorrows: *failure in preaching* and *failure in friendship*. His own, the disciples, the apostles, hadn't assimilated Christ's message with their hearts and it was necessary he should give his life for them. This is the kernel of the Gospel: it was necessary that the Son of God should give up his life so that human beings would be able to grasp the extent of the Father's love.

Introduction to the meditatio

The message of Jesus's life grows gradually clearer: everything moves towards the cross, towards death. We can read this even in *Isaiah 53* and apply it straight to Jesus:

> "Yet it was the will of the Lord to bruise him;
>   he has put him to grief;
> when he makes himself an offering for sin,
>   he shall see his offspring, he shall prolong his days;
> the will of the Lord shall prosper in his hand;
>   he shall see the fruit of the travail of his soul
>   and be satisfied;
> by his knowledge shall the righteous one, my servant,
>   make many to be accounted righteous;
>   and he shall bear their iniquities.
> Therefore I will divide him a portion with the great,
>   and he shall divide the spoil with the strong;
> because he poured out his soul to death,
>   and was numbered with the transgressors;
> yet he bore the sin of many,
>   and made intercession for the transgressors."
>
> (*vv. 10–12*)

Jesus obtained by suffering what he hadn't succeeded in obtaining by teaching.

He was beset with difficulties of every sort, with political and family ordeals, but with death he took all things back into his own hands.

Let us begin our personal meditation and, following St Ignatius's suggestion for the first colloquy after the meditation on our sins, say before Christ Crucified: Behold what you have done for me and what I have done for you (cf *Exercises, n. 53*)

Perhaps Jesus will address David's words to Absalom to you: "O my son, would I had died instead of you!"

And let us ask him in return: Tell me, Lord, what I can do and suffer for you? (cf *ibidem n. 197*).

PASTORAL PATIENCE

(Homily for Saturday in the XVI week "per annum")

'Grant us, Lord, to understand the true application of the parable of the darnel so as not to fall into superficial or convenient interpretations. You alone can enlighten us, for in the history of the Church down through the centuries, various interpretations have been placed upon it. We wish to enter into your heart and your life, so as to grasp the true meaning of your words.'

After the parable of the sower, Jesus tells the crowd the so-called parable of the darnel *(Mt 13:24–30)*. Let us read it again, dividing it into two parts.

— In the first part the facts are set out: the kingdom of heaven is like a man who has sown good seed. During the night his enemy comes and sows darnel all among the wheat. When the plants come up and bear grain, then the darnel appears as well *(vv. 24–26)*.

The facts tell us that good preparations were made but the results were disappointing in respect to the effort expended.

— The second part consists of two questions asked by the servants and two answers given by the master. The servants ask how this strange situation has arisen, and they hear that it's the work of an enemy. They then ask what is to be done, and the master tells them to wait until harvest-time rather than risk uprooting the wheat while weeding out the darnel.

1) In the more general sense, the parable means that not everything goes according to our plans, including our pastoral ones, and in this sense it repeats the teaching in the parable of the sower: you may sow well but the results are not necessarily as good.

Whereas however, for the first sower the drama was played out between the forces of nature — birds, stony ground, thorns — now the drama is played out between people.

Basically the question doesn't change: how can it come about that the darnel springs up? How can it happen that in the Kingdom of God the fruits don't appear that are expected? How can it be that Jesus, having preached so much, did not succeed? Where does the guilt lie?

In the parable the master reassures us by replying that the seed was good and the darnel was not due to the carelessness of the sower, but to the Enemy.

So you see, the Church is not an electronic machine, with which you only have to follow the instructions for use for everything then to work perfectly. The principle is applicable to all our activities: education, pastoral endeavour, catechesis.

We shall not get the results we hope for, because Church life is a perennial confrontation with the Adversary, a life of strife, of battle. Many of the psalms speak to us about enemies, to warn us that in fact human existence is not a calm, straightforward evolution from less to more. We should take the malice of the Enemy into account and this isn't easy to quantify.

If in the years of the novitiate we thought that we should grow from virtue to virtue, with the passing of time we have encountered great difficulties and have had to wage a spiritual battle to overcome the darkness intent on suffocating the light.

Jesus was a man struggling against the Adversary throughout his life, and his example gives us the courage and strength to follow him into the battle.

2) The servants' second question is a more awkward one: *what is to be done?* I say awkward and difficult because it can occur in so many different manners, be it in Church life or in world history.

We could question the divine economy of salvation and ask: Why doesn't God rid the world of the wicked? Scripture replies that only at the end will God's plan be truly revealed, that we haven't yet understood the revelation of the children of God since we haven't yet understood the mystery of the "children of darkness". This being the case, we are in a provisional economy, and this requires us to be very patient. You'll have to wait, says the master in the parable.

The problem becomes even more difficult when we try to apply the teaching to the life of the Church.

Calling to mind Jesus's words about brotherly correction (cf *Mt 18:15f*), we may think that if a brother (or sister for that matter) is repeatedly admonished and still won't listen, we may regard him or her as a pagan and a publican, ripe for expulsion from the community. But doesn't the parable say the darnel isn't to be separated from the good grain?

In my opinion, we as servants of the Church are invited to practice pastoral patience and thus imitate God. Patience isn't the same thing as the bonhomie that accepts anything without drawing distinction. Both St Paul and the evangelist John have very harsh words for those who do not hand on the true teaching of Christ.

We can't draw a mathematical deduction from the parable.

Wiser perhaps to ask how the parable has been interpreted in Church history, and here I should like to mention St Augustine who makes use of this very parable to defend himself against those — the servants' voices, that is to say — who wanted him to be stricter with members of the community at Hippo.

The servants indeed are always around. At certain moments in the life of the Church they are the pure, the fervent, the *élites* who insist Christianity is a very serious religion and we should close the doors, only hanging on to those of the faithful who are right-minded and prepared to make great sacrifices.

The Bishops find themselves embarrassingly placed when they hear talk of this sort. They admire the fervent souls fighting for a lovelier, holier concept of the Church, they esteem them, but will it be right to lean entirely on a little flock and send everyone else away?

Here I want to refer once more to Augustine who, at the end of the fourth century and the beginning of the fifth, was living through a situation somewhat similar to our own: many people wanted to be baptised because the Christian religion had become fashionable and Christians enjoyed a privileged position in society.

So, in the community at Hippo, there were people who didn't go to church regularly, others who went without any sort of commitment, others yet again who didn't put into practice the teachings they had received. Augustine was aware of the fact that these Christians were a dead-weight for the Church.

What does he do? He meditates on the parable of the darnel and decides to wait, to be patient, to go on helping the people without claiming startling results. His decision isn't the fruit of negligence, or laziness, or convenience; it is based rather on faith in God's patience.

3)   In conclusion, I think we should pray a lot and reflect at length, so as to grasp how the parable is to be interpreted at a given moment in history. The decision then must be left to the mind of the Church and the responsibility of the pastors.

Certainly, there will always be divergences between the pure, the fervent, the *élites*, and the more patient. Pastors are called, as St Augustine was, to find the right path. This is not to say that if, faced with a situation, the Bishop should choose meekness and the compromise solution, all is then allowable. It simply means that judgement is left to God and, from the pastoral point of view, for the good of all the grain, the waiting way is the one to take.

I personally prefer, at least in times like ours, the solution adopted by St Augustine, and he is a good model, however things may be.

In any case we ought to pray unceasingly to the Lord to give us his light, so that we can find a right balance between rigidity, severity, and a gentleness that does justice to the living force of the Gospel and God's love.

12

The cross of the Risen Christ, the key to history

'Lord, our God and our Father, we ask you for the knowledge of the cross of your Son.

Grant us to contemplate him as John the faithful witness contemplated him, as the first Christians contemplated him, and Stephen in the last moments of his life. Grant, Father, that we may contemplate the glory which you have given to your Son and which shines forth on the cross, Make us sharers in the contemplation of the holy Fathers of the Church, of the saints and mystics of all ages, of those who have given their lives for the faith and have forgiven those who did them wrong. We ask you this for the sake of Jesus who forgave his enemies, for the sake of Jesus who is the Messiah, the Christ, our Lord who lives and reigns with you in the unity of the Holy Spirit for ever and ever. Amen.'

Our last meditation introduced us to contemplation of the passion and the cross, preferably made on our own before a Crucifix or before the Blessed Sacrament, while slowly reading over a few biblical passages.

I should just like to help your contemplation by reminding you of a passage in the *Letter to the Hebrews* which we have already considered. Indeed all our reflections have been an attempt to elucidate the Christology contained in this letter, so as to acquire — in the spirit of St Ignatius's *Exercises* — true knowledge of God's will shining forth in Christ Jesus the Universal King.

I should therefore like to take a careful second look at the opening two verses of chapter 12: "Therefore, since we are surrounded by so great a cloud of witnesses, let us also lay aside every weight, and sin which clings so closely, and let us run with perseverance the race that is set before us, looking to Jesus the pioneer and perfecter of our faith, who for the joy that was set before him endured the cross, despising the shame, and is seated at the right hand of the throne of God" (*Heb 12:1–2*).

The passage as a whole (cf also *vv. 3–4*) is an exhortation, a message to a community in danger of turning in on itself, of becoming sickly — a community which perhaps hadn't seen its hopes of earlier days fulfilled and was consequently wondering if it was still on the right track. The author's advice is to persevere in the race, to put up a fight, not to give in.

Linguistically speaking, the entire Letter centres round the name of Jesus: all things converge on and derive from him. At the very beginning we are told that Jesus "reflects the glory of God and bears the very stamp of his nature" (*1:3*).

However, this is the Jesus promised in the Old Testament, promised to David, perfecting the virtues, the attitudes, the ordeals of the human king beloved and chosen by God, just as he brings the entire Old Testament to perfection.

We shall halt, by way of introduction, at Jesus. Then we shall comment on the key-words of the first two verses of chapter 12 — cloud of witnesses, weight, ordeal, fixing our gaze, perfection and cross, seated at God's right hand — the better to understand the truth about Jesus himself.

Lastly, we shall ask ourselves what the message is for us today.

Introduction

For the *Letter to the Hebrews*, Jesus is clearly the *Son* by means of whom God has spoken in these last days, the Son who is the heir of all things and upholds the universe by the power of his word (cf *1:1–14*).

This Son is the object of the prophecies, leading us to him as to someone who is a human being and yet superior to all other human beings.

The prophecies quoted in the *Letter* are all in the Davidic tradition: "For to what angel did God ever say, 'I will be to him a father, and he shall be to me a son'?" (*1:5*). The first passage represents the prophetic tradition running back to *Psalm 110*, which Jesus himself attributes to David when he says: "How is it then that David, inspired by the Spirit, calls him Lord, saying, 'The Lord said to my Lord, Sit at my right hand, till I put thy enemies under thy feet?' " (*Mt 22:43–44*).

The second passage exactly repeats *2 Samuel 7:14*: "I will be to him a father, and he shall be to me a son".

There is a further reference to the royal, messianic, Davidic tradition to be found in *v. 8*: "Thy throne, O God, is for ever and ever; the righteous sceptre is the sceptre of thy kingdom", words recalling *Psalm 45*.

Again, in *v. 13*: "But to what angel has he ever said, 'Sit at my right hand, till I make thy enemies a stool for thy feet'?" Here the quotation from *Psalm 110* turns up again, also to be used in Peter's sermon demonstrating that David is the type and promise of Jesus (cf *Acts 2:34–35*).

We can therefore understand the Jesus of the opening verses of chapter 12 in this sense: he is the fulfilment of the Davidic, messianic, prophetic hope of the Old Testament.

The cloud of witnesses

We can now reflect on those words in the verses, first of which is: cloud of witnesses. What does this mean? We have already mentioned it but now the time has come to try and understand it more comprehensively. It is the troop of witnesses of chapter 11, who represent the way of Old Testament faith. Jesus is the first principle, restorer and perfecter of that faith.

At the very beginning, the Bible shows us the way of life and human beings almost immediately entering the way of death. The way of life, that is to say, God's will, is that human beings should live and so, when human beings fall, God saves them by putting them back on the right path by means of faith.

The way of faith is the entire Old Testament: human beings, who cannot be saved by the direct way of life, enter by the way of faith.

The way of faith is thus a kind of confidence in God, of surrender to him, to his word, to his plan of salvation.

The two ways — that of faith and that of death — are the key to all Scripture and also to the *Spiritual Exercises*.

The way of faith begins with Abel, the first righteous man; the author of the *Letter to the Hebrews* then describes all the other patriarchs who travelled the way of salvation in obedience to God's new design. This plan did not in itself contain perfection, since their faith was to be completed in Jesus.

Chapter 11 is a very fine summary, viewing the Bible as a unity, as a journey, in which to learn to practise faith, which God requires his people to perform. Unfortunately it only mentions David in passing, listing him with Gideon, Barak, Samson, Jephthah and Samuel. Even so, in the general description we find many features of his own story: he conquered kingdoms, meted out justice, showed valour in war, repelled invading enemies (cf *11:33*).

The chapter ends by affirming that none of those great models of faith received what was promised, since God had something better in mind, which was that they were not to reach perfection except with us (*v. 39*).

It is therefore right to admire the faith, virtue, sufferings of the ancients, but this is not all.

For now we too have joined this people of faith, journeying in the world, in this universe of spiritually very rich men and women; we have taken our places in God's grand design.

There is a cloud of witnesses accompanying us, suffering and praying for us: the grand movement of the people of the living God, marching towards final victory, to eternal life, the eschatological age.

Throwing off the weight and running the race

Having entered the cloud of witnesses, what ought we to do once the path takes definite shape and is completed in the perfect faith of Jesus? The author of the *Letter* exhorts us:

— First, *we should throw off everything that weighs us down* (cf *12:1*) and the sin that clings to us so closely.

This is the programme of the *Spiritual Exercises* conceived as an episode in salvation history, as part of the Bible, as mankind making choice of the way of God.

Faith puts us back on the way of life, but to enter we must rid ourselves of every disordered affection, throw away everything in our lives that isn't ordered: that's the first week of the *Exercises*.

For exegetes the meaning of the term *weighs us down* is obvious: to make headway you have to be free, not be impeded by worldliness and vanity.

Less easy to understand is the term *sin*, since in Greek this is *euperìstaton 'amartìan*, which literally would mean the sin that is near us in a positive way. Obviously this problem is the delight of textual critics; among many conjectural readings, a particularly interesting one would be to read *euperìspaston* for *euperìstaton*, which does in fact occur in the third century Papyrus 46. Instead of *'amartìan*, one would read *'apartìan*. The translation would then be: load that would be useful.

This is another way of pointing out that, having to run, we need to free ourselves of everything. And indeed immediately afterwards it says: "and run with perseverance the race" (*v. 1*). Not however win the race, but run it. The race is the sign of fervour. As you see, the verse isn't easy to interpret. What is sure is that the author insists on the need to undertake the way of perfection.

"Running with perseverance the race that is set before us" is the task for the second week of the *Exercises*, which we have been trying to complete: contemplating Jesus's virtues, his way of behaving, the poverty he experienced.

Fixing our gaze — perfection of faith — cross

We have reached the moment of decision:

"Fixing our eyes on Jesus the pioneer and perfecter

of our faith, who for the joy that was set before him, endured the cross" (*v. 2*).

This is a passage very rich in meaning.

— *"Fixing our gaze"* is an expression immediately taking us back to the prophecy quoted by John: "They shall look on him whom they have pierced" (*Jn 19:37*).

The faithful witness, the disciple more beloved than any other, has grasped, by fixing his gaze on Christ Crucified, the meaning of Jesus's entire life and teaching.

Contemplation of the passion shows us the fulfilment of the Old Testament: all the ordeals undergone by David and the other Old Testament saints find their perfection in the cross of Jesus. It follows that the cross is the perfection of the history of mankind, of the history of cultures and civilisations: the cross is the key to history.

— *"On the pioneer of our faith"*. The faith of the patriarchs had a leader; to the majority of them he remained invisible, but Moses, for instance, glimpsed him, looked to him, regulating his choices by his mysterious contemplation of the Christ. "By faith Moses, when he was grown up, refused to be called the son of Pharaoh's daughter, choosing rather to share ill-treatment with the people of God than to enjoy the fleeting pleasures of sin. He considered *abuse suffered for the Christ* greater wealth than the treasures of Egypt" (*Heb 11:24–26*).

— The concept that *Jesus perfects the faith* we may consider a little more extensively, since it is fundamental to the whole *Letter*. The subject is broached where it says: "It was fitting that he, for whom and by whom all things exist, in bringing many sons to glory, should make the pioneer of their salvation *perfect* through suffering" (*2:10*).

The leader becomes perfect by means of the cross and thus guides all to perfection, offering the true key for understanding human nature, history, civilisations, cultures.

Christ's perfection lies in his choosing the cross for the sake of the joy that lay ahead of him.

The third degree of humility proposed by St Ignatius consists in choosing the way of the cross, so as to be like and with Jesus (cf *Exercises n. 167*).

The Crucified One resurrected and seated at God's right hand

The second verse of Chapter 12 ends by stating that this Jesus who disregarded the shame of the cross *has taken his seat at the right hand of God.*

Cross and glory will never more be separated, and indeed the same evangelist John contemplates the Crucified One, radiant with glory, in the act of bestowing the Spirit.

I should like to remind you of a passage in the *Acts of the Apostles*, which may serve as a commentary on *Hebrews 12:2*.

Stephen has delivered his speech to the Sanhedrin, rousing everybody's anger: "When they heard these things, they were enraged and ground their teeth against him" (*Acts 7:54*).

He is now faced with a choice. To avoid being stoned to death, he can deny Jesus, as Peter did. "But he, full of the Holy Spirit, gazed into heaven and saw the glory of God, and Jesus standing at the right hand of God; and he said, 'Behold, I see the heavens opened, and the Son of man standing at the right hand of God' " (*Acts 7:55–56*).

Each word has its meaning.

"*Gazing into heaven*". By the grace of the Holy Spirit, he succeeds in detaching himself from the situation and danger he is in, going into a sort of ecstasy.

"He saw the glory of God", that glory representing all the yearnings of the Old Testament.

"*And Jesus standing at the right hand of God; and he said, 'Behold, I see the heavens opened, and the Son of man standing at the right hand of God.' *" He sees Jesus in the glory of God but as Son of man, as the Crucified One resurrected, as the head of the Church, who hasn't yet handed the kingdom back to the Father because he is waiting for the whole innumerable army of men and women of every century to come to him.

This is why he is *standing*, not seated.

Contemplating the Crucified One resurrected, for Stephen, clarifies the meaning of his life and he has no further doubts about what to choose: he wills to reach perfection of faith.

On hearing these words, the assembly broke into wild shouting, rushed at him, thrust him out of the city and started to stone him (cf *7:57–58*).

— "As they were stoning Stephen, he prayed, 'Lord Jesus, receive my spirit' " (*7:59*).

This is the first expression of perfection of faith. Jesus ended his own life by committing it in complete confidence into the Father's hands. And he it is who has now led Stephen to the peak of love, self-surrender, perfection of faith.

Clearly we intend, through Jesus's faith, to surrender ourselves completely to God, and in this sense he is the leader. He possesses it in perfect manner and makes us sharers in it.

Forthwith Stephen comes to repeat his very words: Father, receive my spirit!

— "Then he knelt down and cried with a loud voice, 'Lord, *do not hold this sin against them*' " (*7:60*).

This is the other expression of the faith that has reached perfection: forgiveness, the perfect gift. A gift unknown to David and the whole Old Testament, forgiveness was inaugurated by Jesus.

The cross is the perfection of human history, since it reveals the end of the entire process of vertical transcendence of human nature, that is to say, faith; and the culmination of the entire process of horizontal transcendence of human nature, that is to say, forgiveness.

From Davidic kingship to prophetic interpretation, Jesus brings all to perfection. His love for God to the point of self-giving and his love for others to the point of forgiving become the definitive key to history.

He has truly brought forth "justice for the nations" (cf *Is 42:1*), for justice is the cross understood as the perfection of faith and love.

The message for us

The way of faith is hard, it costs us great effort to live it.

Even so, it is important to know all about it, so as not to fall into the error, especially today, of confusing it with the way of a given civilisation.

The way of faith is totally original and is the touchstone for every culture, which will hence be judged by its light.

But for all that, it is extremely difficult to preach and present a faith which is completed on the cross.

The cross cannot be presented with arrogance, how much less can one presume to impose it. One cannot impose the charity that goes as far as self-giving, as far as forgiving, as far as the perfect gift, with absolutely no strings attached.

We shall have to present it as Jesus did, as David did who bore witness to it, indirectly, by the many trials that made up his life: with humility, with gentleness, by example.

Charity is indeed taught by loving; forgiveness is taught by forgiving. And in history there is no higher form of perfection than this.

We shall have to contemplate this as a height to which the Spirit of Jesus alone can bring us, and this is why we are encouraged to pray a great deal and continually confront the reality of the cross.

So I suggest two questions for you:

1) Do we know how to forgive sincerely? Ability to forgive someone isn't written in our own story as human beings, but in Jesus's story.

'Lord Jesus, steady us day by day on the way of faith, in your way of the cross. We believe in you, in the blood you shed on the cross, and we want to let ourselves be invaded by love for you; we want to contemplate you in your resplendent beauty. Give us the Holy Spirit, so that he may teach us this charity.'

2) Do we know how to accept forgiveness from others? Perhaps this is harder than asking to be forgiven. Jesus asks us to learn how to receive absolutely free forgiveness from someone else, to bring us to perfection by the way of faith.

13

David's ideal: Jesus's ideal: the people of God's ideal

'We thank you, God our Father, for having raised your Son Jesus Christ to life for us and for having inaugurated the new life of this age in which we wait for his coming.

Grant us to contemplate the face of the Risen One in your Church; make us available to the action of the Holy Spirit as he builds up the body of your Risen Son until such time as he presents it to you at the end of the ages, so that you may be all in all.

Father, in Jesus you have given us an ultimate, definitive ideal to illuminate every single moment of the human journey: an ideal that corresponds to the deepest longings, deepest needs of mankind, to the truest sufferings of the men and women of our times. We ask you to make us contemplate this ideal through Jesus, the better for us to serve your plan of salvation.'

The contemplations in the fourth week of St Ignatius's *Exercises* are among the most difficult ones, since they concern meditating on Jesus, who is near us but no longer among us: with asking, that is to say, for the grace "to be intensely glad and to rejoice in the great glory and joy of Christ our Lord" (*n. 221*).

In another way, meditating on the life of the Risen Christ involves entering into the permanent economy of the Church. St Ignatius's last great contemplation is indeed the "contemplation for obtaining love" (cf *nn. 230–235*), that is to say, to see the Risen Christ present everywhere, to see the Church journeying and being built up through the centuries, to see the Spirit resurrecting Jesus in the hearts of the faithful.

If we have the eye of faith, we recognise God's design; if we do not, we regard many of the events and moments in our lives and in the Church's life as commonplace and negative. To help you in your contemplation of the Risen Jesus, I thought I would outline a meditation for you, to be called: David's ideal, Jesus's ideal, God's people's ideal.

Introduction

The *ideal* is that which represents for you, or is offered to you as, a perfect type or absolute model. From a subjective point of view, it is what, in a certain order of things, would perfectly satisfy the aspirations of my heart and spirit.

I speak of an historical ideal, of a situation which at least in part can be realised in this world.

Even so, no historical ideal can prescind from the eschatological absolute: the quest for penultimate or antepenultimate ideals would have no meaning without reference to that definitive one.

The absolute eschatological ideal can be expressed in a variety of ways.

— Theologically it is known as *the beatific vision*, to see God face to face as Jesus sees the Father. Hence to be with Jesus before the Father's face, by the grace of the Spirit, for ever.

— The *heavenly Jerusalem* is a most beautiful image, a magnificent symbol of the ultimate ideal (*Rev 21*).

— In *Romans 8:11*, St Paul expresses it as the *final resurrection* of all the righteous.

— Or again, in *1 Corinthians 15:28*, the absolute eschatological ideal is the *kingdom handed over to the Father*: "When all things are subjected to him, then the Son himself will also be subjected to him who put all things under him, that God may be everything to every one". A little earlier, the Apostle has pointed out that without this hope in eternal life, no historical ideal would mean anything: "If for this life only we had hoped in Christ, we are of all men most to be pitied" (*v. 19*).

The question I put to myself in this meditation is as

follows: Starting from the heavenly Jerusalem, can one specify any visible, social reflections of the final resurrection in history? In the interval between the resurrection of Jesus and the general resurrection of the just, what ideals for realising the Kingdom can one specify?

Let us first consider David, then Jesus and lastly the people of God.

David's ideal

What was David's historical ideal? What did he glimpse as the absolute model for the realisation of his and his people's wishes.

It isn't hard to find out what it was, set down whether explicitly or implicitly in the *Books of Samuel*, as also in many passages in the *Psalms*, conveying David's longings and aspirations in the form of prayer.

1) The fundamental text, which we have already studied, is *2 Samuel 7*.

The Lord has promised him a house and, after the prophet Nathan has passed on all God's words to him, David begins his prayer: "Who am I, O Lord God, and what is my house, that thou hast brought me thus far?" (*v. 18*).

What the Lord has already given him is amazing: he has taken him from the pastures where he was following the flocks, has made him leader of the people, has made him victorious in battle, has given him stability and peace for Israel.

David's ideal is thus: kingdom, peace, prosperity, safety from enemies, joy, dancing in the temple. The king is happy, perfectly satisfied. "And yet this was a small thing in thy eyes, O Lord God; thou has spoken also of thy servant's house for a great while to come . . . O Lord God!" (*v. 19*).

At *v. 19* we therefore have a second important aspect of this ideal: all that has come about already — kingdom, peace, prosperity and so forth — will continue into the future, is stable.

David can't imagine desiring more and indeed in *vv. 28–29* was to exclaim: "And now, O Lord God, thou art God, and thy words are true, and thou hast promised this good thing to thy servant; now therefore may it please thee to bless the house of thy servant, that it may continue for ever before thee; for thou, O Lord God, hast spoken, and with thy blessing shall the house of thy servant be blessed for ever''.

2) All the same, this ideal, seeming to crown David's every possible wish, only comes about in part: neither kingly office nor the divine promise give the king a happy life. Chapter 9, following close on the great prayer, has for title, in the *Jerusalem Bible*: "David's family and the intrigues over the succession''.

A number of very painful vicissitudes both domestic and social are recounted, culminating in his son Absalom's rebellion and death. The ideal is there but remains in the background, and from the Psalms we learn that David goes beyond, expresses higher aspirations, grasps that there is something better than kingdom and peace. "O God, thou art my God, I seek thee, my soul thirsts for thee . . . thy steadfast love is better than life" (*Ps 63:1, 3*). The ideal is to be close to God. Perhaps David doesn't grasp how one can be close to God without peace, kingdom, temple, yet he feels that this is so. "Do not thou, O Lord, withhold thy mercy from me, let thy steadfast love and thy faithfulness ever preserve me!" (*Ps 40:11*). God is greater than the kingdom, since he is the author of all prosperity, all peace, all kingdom. He is in himself good, marvellous, rich in joy: "May all who seek thee rejoice and be glad in thee; may those who love thy salvation say continually, 'Great is the Lord!' " (*Ps 40:16*).

This tension present in the Psalms still helps us to pray today. If it only concerned the ideal of an earthly kingdom, the Psalter would not be of universal application. There is this messianic reaching out towards the absolute ideal of history, though in the Old Testament it is never completely clear what the ideal is, in spite of there being a number of very exalted, climactic moments, as in *Isaiah 11*: "There shall come forth a shoot from the stump of Jesse, and a branch shall grow out of his roots. And the Spirit of the Lord shall rest upon him, the spirit of wisdom and understanding, the spirit of counsel and might, the spirit of knowledge and the fear of the Lord. . . . They shall not hurt or destroy in all my holy mountain; for the earth shall be full of the knowledge of the Lord as the waters cover the sea'' (*vv. 1–2, 9*).

Thus we see that for David and the Davidic dynasty, the acme of the ideal was a kingdom of absolute peace, in the knowledge of God, in concord among human beings, in harmony with all creation.

Jesus's ideal

— Jesus expresses his historical ideal in one word especially, and this harks faithfully back to David: the *Kingdom*.

Unless we know what David's ideal was, we cannot grasp the full significance of Jesus's.

Jesus starts out from this concept and keeps taking it up and enriching it in his parables, discourses and responses. At *Matthew 4:17*, where it is said that Jesus begins to preach the need for repentance ''for the kingdom of heaven is at hand'', the *Jerusalem Bible* has a note that admirably sums up all the New Testament data on the Kingdom. It would certainly be useful for every one of you to have a look at it.

Thenceforward he speaks continuously about his historical ideal, even after the resurrection: ''appearing to them during forty days and speaking of the Kingdom of God'' (*Acts 1:3*).

But Jesus always mixes the historical ideal with the eschatological one, so that his preaching isn't easy to interpret. He announces a definitive, absolute Kingdom, which however begins now, affects human beings, changes the way people relate to one another, has the primacy of peace and forgiveness. And in this world the Kingdom has certain dark aspects, of suffering and humiliation, which require contemplation of the final Kingdom before they can be understood and accepted.

— This key-word is not the only one, since Jesus's

ideal transcends rigid terminology and adopts various kinds of language.

In *John 17*, he asks the Father, in prayer, for what he most desires with the depths of his being. We too, when we want something very much, ask for it in prayer: if we ask for physical health, this means that being healthy is our ideal at that moment; if we ask for peace in the Church, it means that peace of this kind is our ideal.

What does Jesus ask for? That the Father should glorify him: "Now, Father, glorify thou me with the glory which I had with thee before the world was made" (*v. 5*).

God's glory is the absolute eschatological ideal of Jesus and he asks it for himself and for all mankind.

But again, in that prayer he expresses an historical ideal: "I do not pray for these alone, but also for those who believe in me through their word, that they may all be one; even as thou, Father, art in me and I in thee, that they also may be in us, *so that the world may believe* that thou hast sent me" (*vv. 20–21*; cf *22–23*).

It is the ideal of the *unity of believers* with him, the unity of those who are his own and of himself with the Father, so that the world may believe. The Kingdom is expressed in the language of unity. We may indeed say that Holy Church is the unity of the Father, the Son and the Holy Spirit realised in this world, it is sharing definitively in human existence.

— *Matthew 28:18–19*: "All authority in heaven and on earth has been given to me. Go therefore and make disciples of all nations in the name of the Father and of the Son and of the Holy Spirit." The ideal of unity in the Trinity is presented as dynamic, missionary. The Church has been entrusted with this historical ideal of Jesus's.

— *Luke 24:45–57*: Jesus opens the apostles' minds to the meaning of the Scriptures, the books of the Old Testament, since it was already written there that he would suffer death and rise again, and that in his name repentance and the forgiveness of sins would be preached to the whole world, "*beginning from Jerusalem*".

This is another way of expressing Jesus's historical ideal.

He mentions the city of David to show that Jerusalem in physical manner represents the community of the promises. And even today Jerusalem is still the first principle of the whole Church's mission: this is a great mystery. We ought always to be spiritually orientated towards the Holy City. Rome represents the local Church as being responsible for, being entrusted with, safeguarding unity, but this doesn't abolish the symbolic significance of Jerusalem as the starting point of the mission to the ends of the earth.

For this reason I think it's very important that today there should be a Judaeo-Christian community in Jerusalem, to make visible, as it were, the Church's connection with the whole of salvation history.

From the texts I have mentioned, it emerges that the Risen Christ presents the synthesis of his ideal. During his life he spoke in enigmas, in parables, or under the mysterious sign of the cross. After the resurrection, he reveals it completely as the *ideal of the unity of mankind in him, in the Church.*

The Church as unity of the human race; the human race as unity before God.

Jesus's approach to teaching the faith is fundamental: he didn't explain everything at once, since he knew that human beings' progress towards unity has to be gradual.

We are invited to follow his example, by taking people's physical situations into account and by helping the individual in a way commensurate with what he or she at a given moment can understand.

The people of God's ideal

It would be a fine thing to leaf through the New Testament and see how many modes the ideal is described in, that Jesus left to his people.

— The word *Kingdom* more or less disappears, having borne so much fruit in the choice of the royal, messianic, Davidic line. Terminology can change henceforth, since what Jesus intended to convey has been understood.

We still find it in *Romans 14:17* but, as it were, in passing, since St Paul was very familiar with the term. The

Apostle is vexed with the problem of clean and unclean foods and says: "The Kingdom of God does not mean food and drink but righteousness and peace and joy in the Holy Spirit". This is typical of the second phase of Pauline preaching. In the first, he preached the eschatological coming of Christ; in the second, the extension of the Kingdom in people's hearts, the Kingdom among human beings: joy, justice, peace, whatever affects the way people live and behave.

The ideal is expressed in the moral reflections of the Kingdom.

— *Galatians 5:22* presents this ideal in deeply personalised terms: "The fruit of the Spirit is love, joy, peace, patience, kindness, goodness, faithfulness, gentleness, self-control".

In history, a people moved by the Spirit is a simple, mild, joyful, humble, pure, kind, patient community. The ideal is thus now stated in precise, specific terms, suited to differing circumstances.

— In the third phase of his preaching, St Paul chooses rather to emphasise this ideal, not so much as proper to the Christian community, but rather as a cosmic ideal embracing the universe. *Ephesians 1:10*: the mystery of God's will, the ideal that is to be realised in history, is to bring everything together under Christ. *Colossians 1:19–20* proclaims Christ as the true and only head: "For in him all the fulness of God was pleased to dwell, and through him to reconcile to himself all things, whether on earth or in heaven, making peace by the blood of his cross". It is the ideal of the body of Christ, growing to the perfect stature of Christ.

The words change, but not the substance. Jesus talked about the banquet, the net; Paul uses various terms, but the basic ideal is always the same, clothing itself in varying language according to the historical moment.

The grace of the Holy Spirit connects the ideal of Jesus to that of Paul, of Peter, of Ambrose, of Augustine, of Gregory the Great, all the way to that of Vatican II.

The important thing to remember is that each set of terms

is always inspired by contemplation of the cross and resurrection, by contemplation of the Crucified and Risen One who is the absolute ideal, the definitive Messiah, the key to history.

— It is therefore interesting to ask how the Church of today proposes to express its ideal, and which images seem best adapted to our times. It seems to me that for us the norm of expression ought to be Vatican II with the wonderful and meaningful documents it has given us.

I want to mention one or two of them since we should always be guided by them in the way we live and express the ideal of the people of God in our preaching.

First of all, the introduction to *Lumen gentium:* Christ is the light of all nations "and by her relationship with Christ, the Church is a kind of sacrament or sign and instrument of intimate union with God and of the unity of all mankind" (*n. 1*). It is a very well found formula for what the Church is in the world, and no other entity can better express the unity of all mankind: the Council gives a prophetic interpretation to the fundamental longing of our times. The young very strongly feel this ideal of unity, reflecting that of the heavenly Jerusalem. It is an historical ideal which can be set before the people of today, at the same time it is irradiated with the ideal of God, who wills to unite the human race in Christ. The Church describes itself rightly as "sacrament or sign".

In *Gaudium et spes* the general ideal is stated more specifically.

The key-text is *n. 45*, which we find halfway through the constitution. It is somewhat like *Mark 8:27–30* — the confession of Peter — round which all the rest of the gospel revolves.

"While helping the world and receiving many benefits from it, the Church has a single intention: that God's Kingdom may come and that the salvation of the whole human race may come to pass . . . *The Lord is the goal of human history,* 'the focal point of the longings of history and of civilisation', the centre of the human race, the joy of every heart and the answer to all its yearnings".

This sort of Christological confession of the Church is taken from an allocution of Paul VI, delivered on February 3, 1965, and has been deliberately placed at the centre of the document.

Then again, this ideal is expressed in terms of *peace*. "The name of peace today is development", Paul VI was to say. "The new name for peace is solidarity", John Paul II echoes his words.

The conciliar text affirms: "Moving gradually together and everywhere more conscious already of its oneness, this family cannot accomplish its task of constructing for all men everywhere a world more genuinely human, unless each person devotes himself with renewed determination to the reality of peace" (*n. 77*). An historical ideal corresponding to the Davidic kingdom: peace, security for all, but extended to the entire world. "Thus it happens that the gospel message, which is in harmony with the loftier strivings and aspirations of the human race, takes on a new lustre in our day as it declares that the artisans of peace are blessed 'for they shall be called children of God' " (*ibidem*).

And again: "That earthly peace which arises from love of neighbour symbolises and results from the peace of Christ, who comes forth from the Father" (*n. 78*).

It is not a matter of confusing the realities but rather of keeping the opening absolutely clear, the debouchment as it were, of the historical ideal: earthly peace is the image and effect of the peace of God in Christ. The definitive peace proclaimed by the Church is indeed related to peace on earth.

Lastly, *Gaudium et spes* points up the historical ideal by referring to the *family of nations* and to *international agencies*: "Today the bonds of mutual dependence become increasingly close between all citizens and all the peoples of the world. The universal common good needs to be intelligently pursued and more effectively achieved. Hence it is now necessary for the family of nations to create for themselves an order which corresponds to modern obligations, particularly with reference to those numerous regions still labouring under intolerable need. For the attainment of these goals, agencies of the international community should do their part, to provide for the various necessities of men'' (*n. 84*).

This is also the basic theme of the more recent encyclical *Sollicitudo rei socialis.*

The definitive Christian hope is still the same: peace, inner righteousness, the presence of God, the Holy Spirit prompting the human heart; the Church however helps us to give this an historical content, to put it in a context of historical and social irradiation which takes account of the miseries of the world, of the inequalities, of the dangers of war, of the sufferings of the poor.

We are thus invited to convey these realities into an always difficult unity, to which we must commit ourselves as servants of God's grand design.

Conclusion

The grace to ask for, in this contemplation, is to be able to fix our gaze on the Risen Christ in such way as not to be divided in heart, either as individuals or as Church, between the absolute eschatological ideal and historical ideals, between prayer and the inner life on the one hand, and pastoral responsibilities and apostolic labour on the other.

Only contemplation of Jesus can make us grasp the end point of the story, the fulfilment of each deeper aspiration, and consequently make us understand how each historical ideal receives its own order and how each vocation has its place in the marvellous cosmic design of salvation.

14

David's roots

'God our Father, you allow us to glimpse the end of all history, Jesus the risen Christ, the heavenly Jerusalem, the reunification of peoples, in your covenant for all eternity. Grant us therefore also to understand the roots of this historical movement, so that, in its beginnings, in the small events of every day, we may grasp that which is already present as a pledge of that which is to come. Grant us that unfailing hope that draws us towards you, crowning us with joy. We ask it through Jesus Christ your Son our Lord. Amen.'

We have reached the last meditation of our Exercises. Having tried to deepen our knowledge about the figure of David, I now raise the following question: Is there an infancy story for David in Scripture, as there is for Samuel, for John the Baptist and for Jesus? Obviously I'm not thinking of a childhood chronicle, though that would certainly be interesting, but rather of the atmosphere surrounding the earliest years of Samuel and more particularly the infancy of Jesus. Luke's gospel, for instance, gives us a description of Mary's simplicity, gentleness, humility, spirit of acceptance.

Is it possible to glimpse similar roots of simplicity, humility, gentleness in the story of David?

As I see it, the biblical text containing these is the *Book of Ruth*, a short and very beautiful book. For admission to the Biblical Institute, I recall, we had to have a really good knowledge of the Hebrew text and be prepared to translate any passage set before us.

So in this meditation I suggest we contemplate the story of David beginning with his great-grandmother, all the more particularly since Matthew mentions Ruth at the beginning of his gospel as being an ancestress of Jesus, thus showing her importance for the New Testament: "Salmon was the father of Boaz by Rahab, and Boaz the father of Obed by Ruth, and Obed the father of Jesse, and Jesse the father of David the king" (*1:5*).

Let us see if in the *Book of Ruth* we can discover the spiritual roots of David's career, and hence a message with value for us. As you know, in the Hebrew Scriptures, *Ruth* was not placed among the historical books but was one of the five scrolls, the *Megillot*, which were read on principal feastdays. *Ruth* served for the feast of Pentecost, since its heroine was greatly revered by the people of Israel.

First however let us consider the background to the book: King Moab, Israel's enemy; then we shall look at the five main sections of the book; finally we shall ask ourselves what Ruth represents.

Moab

Ruth is a Moabitess, the daughter of an incestuous people (cf *Gen 19:30–38*) which was to lead Israel into idolatry.

Moab is hence the enemy, one of the names of enemies *par excellence*, determined to destroy Jacob for ever, as Balaam himself was to say: "From Aram Balak has brought me, the king of Moab from the eastern mountains: 'Come, curse Jacob for me, and come, denounce Israel?' " (*Num 23:7*).

God's people were aware of this and were always to remember Moab as a terrible adversary of whom to beware: "He whose testicles are crushed or whose male member is cut off shall not enter the assembly of the Lord.

No bastard shall enter the assembly of the Lord; even to the tenth generation none of his descendants shall enter the assembly of the Lord.

No Ammonite or Moabite shall enter the assembly of the Lord; even to the tenth generation none belonging to them shall enter the assembly of the Lord for ever; because they did not meet you with bread and with water on the way, when you came forth out of Egypt, and because they hired against you Balaam the son of Beor from Pethor of Mesopotamia, to curse you. Nevertheless the Lord your God would not hearken to Balaam; but the Lord your God turned the curse into a blessing for you, because the Lord your God loved you. You shall not seek their peace or their prosperity all your days for ever" (*Deut 23:1–7*).

Even in the days of Nehemiah they still preserved the memory of these two events: "On that day they read from the book of Moses in the hearing of the people; and in it was found written that no Ammonite or Moabite should ever enter the assembly of God; for they did not meet the children of Israel with bread and water, but hired Balaam against them to curse them—yet our God turned the curse into a blessing" (*Neh 13:1–3*). And then Nehemiah explains how he acted: "In those days also I saw the Jews who had married women of Ashdod, Ammon, and Moab; and half of their children spoke the language of Ashdod, and they could not speak the language of Judah, but the language of each people. And I contended with them and cursed them and beat some of them and pulled out their hair; and I made them take oath in the name of God, saying, 'You shall not give your daughters to their sons, or take their daughters for your sons or for yourselves. Did not Solomon king of Israel sin on account of such women? Among the many nations there was no king like him, and he was beloved by his God, and God made him king over all Israel; nevertheless foreign women made even him to sin. Shall we then listen to you and do all this great evil and act treacherously against our God by marrying foreign women?" Nehemiah concludes by boasting of what he has done: "Remember me, O my God, for good!" (*vv. 23–27,31*).

His great undertaking had been that of driving out all the Moabite women.

The Hebrew people's hostility to Moab is also to be found in the Psalms; for instance, *Psalm 108* where disdain is underlined with some elegance: "Moab is my washbasin!" (*v. 9*).

This then is the context in which the delightful *Book of Ruth* is to be read, as a kind of prophecy making a

Moabitess the great-grandmother of King David and ancestress of the Messiah.

Ruth

I suggest a few points for special attention in the five sections into which the book can be divided.

1) The first scene is sited in the countryside of Moab. A man of Bethlehem had been forced to emigrate with his wife Naomi and his two sons because of the famine that had broken out in Judaea. The man dies, his two sons marry two Moabite women, Orpah and Ruth. After a few years the two sons die too and the three women are left without a future.

Having heard that the Lord has given his people food once more, Naomi decides to go home and sets out with her two daughters-in-law on the return journey to Judaea. Prompted however by love for Orpah and Ruth, she says: "Go, return each of you to her mother's house. May the Lord deal kindly with you, as you have dealt with the dead and with me. The Lord grant that you may find a home, each of you in the house of her husband!" Then she kissed them, and they lifted up their voices and wept. And they said to her, "No, we will return with you to your people." But Naomi said, "Turn back, my daughters, why will you go with me? Have I yet sons in my womb that they may become your husbands? Turn back, my daughters, go your way, for I am too old to have a husband. If I should say I have hope, even if I should have a husband this night and should bear sons, would you therefore wait till they were grown? Would you therefore refrain from marrying? No, my daughters, for it is exceedingly bitter to me for your sake that the hand of the Lord has gone forth against me." Then they lifted up their voices and wept again; and Orpah kissed her mother-in-law, but Ruth clung to her.

And she said, "See, your sister-in-law has gone back to her people and to her gods; return after your sister-in-law." But Ruth said, "Entreat me not to leave you or to return from following you; for where you go I will go, and where you lodge I will lodge; your people shall be my people, and your God my God; where you die I will die, and there will I be buried. May the Lord do so to me and more also if even death parts me from you" (*1:8–17*).

The passage is particularly beautiful and gets better as it goes on: there is Naomi's very humane love and Ruth's love, faithful unto death. Ruth's love leads her to a difficult choice: she chooses Naomi's people and her God. Probably she doesn't realise what such a choice will involve, although she is aware of not being able to belong to Israel, of not being able to marry again and have children. Hers is a totally unconditional love, open to faith. Not an explicit faith in God, but a certain awareness of him, responding to the love that God has put in her heart.

2) The account continues by showing that her choice of the God of Israel and of his people is followed by great devotion and service to another.

Very poor, the women have nothing to eat, but Ruth doesn't lean on her mother-in-law and say: Go and look up your friends and ask them for something for us to eat. She goes out to work herself.

We are in Bethlehem at the time of the barley harvest, and Ruth the Moabitess turns to Naomi: " 'Let me go to the field, and glean among the ears of grain after him in whose sight I shall find favour'. And she said to her, 'Go, my daughter' ". Ruth "gleaned in the field until evening; then she beat out what she had gleaned, and it was about an ephah of barley" (*2:2,17*).

The Moabitess asks for nothing; she submits to the laws of Israel; "When you reap your harvest in your field, and have forgotten a sheaf in the field, you shall not go back to get it; it shall be for the sojourner, the fatherless, and the widow" (*Deut 24:19*). She lives humbly in a spirit of service and devotion to her mother-in-law.

3) Ruth's goodness and humility find their counterpart in the kindness and courtesy of Boaz, a man of faith and heart. Of faith because he gives the blessing prescribed in the Psalms: "And behold, Boaz came from Bethlehem; and he said to the reapers, 'The Lord be with

you!' And they answered, 'The Lord bless you!' " (*2:4*; cf
Ps 129:7–8). The entire episode takes place in an atmosphere
of great faith and religious feeling.

Boaz then sees the young woman, asks who she is and
is informed she is a Moabitess and so destined to remain
on the margins of society. Next, Boaz approaches her:
"Listen, my daughter, do not go to glean in another field
or leave this one, but keep close to my maidens" (*v. 8*). The
conversation between Boaz and Ruth is rich in human feeling and deserves careful meditation, since it evokes those
attitudes which are the fruit of the Spirit: "love, joy, peace,
patience, kindness, goodness, faithfulness, gentleness" (*Gal
5:22*). The atmosphere is rather like that in the first two
chapters of St Luke's gospel.

4) The fourth section of the book is about the love
that dawns between Boaz and Ruth with the help of wise
Naomi. Ruth makes herself look her best, perfumes herself,
wraps herself in a cloak and, after dark, goes and lies down
at Boaz's feet, where he sleeps among the heaps of barley.
When the man wakes up comes encounter and recognition:
"May you be blessed by the Lord, my daughter; you have
made this last kindness greater than the first, in that you
have not gone after young men, whether poor or rich. And
now, my daughter, do not fear, I will do for you all that
you ask, for all my fellow townsmen know that you are a
woman of worth" (*3:10–11*).

5) The marriage contract is drawn up without a hitch.
Boaz discharges the duty of meeting a male relative of
Naomi's, who by law has right of redemption over the field
belonging to Naomi's late husband and hence over Ruth
too. The man renounces his right of redemption before
witnesses. Boaz declares himself willing to take the man's
place and the elders conclude it all by saying: "May the Lord
make the woman who is coming into your house, like Rachel
and Leah, who together built up the house of Israel" (*4–11*).
This verse is all-important since it speaks of the wife of
Jacob; Rachel, as you will know, was buried at Bethlehem
where her tomb still stands. "May you prosper in Ephrathah
and be renowned in Bethlehem; and may your house be like

the house of Perez, whom Tamar bore to Judah, because of the children that the Lord will give you by this young woman''.

So Boaz took Ruth and she became his wife; and he went in to her, and the Lord gave her conception, and she bore a son (*vv. 11–13*). Thus Ruth begins to be part of that people whom she, prompted by a sense of faith, had chosen for love of Naomi, and is blessed by the God whom she did not know. Naomi called the boy Obed: "he was the father of Jesse, the father of David.

Now these are the descendants of Perez: Perez was the father of Hezron, Hezron of Ram, Ram of Amminadab, Ammin adab of Nahshon, Nahshon of Salmon, Salmon of Boaz, Boaz of Obed, Obed of Jesse, and Jesse of David'' (*vv. 17–22*).

So the book ends with its double emphasis on her descendant, David. Ruth the Moabitess who should have been shut out for ever from the Chosen People ("none of their descendants even to the tenth generation" cf *Deut 23:3*) becomes a participant in the assembly of the Lord, of the royal, messianic, Davidic line of Judah.

The message of Ruth

First of all, *Ruth is a woman of great faith and great courage*. She is the figure of faith in God and in the future of his people. She is a symbol of the free gift of self to God, and he in turn will never forsake whoever has made this offering. She represents the beginning of David's faith and has her place in that mysterious way of faith, described in the *Letter to the Hebrews*, which was to find its completion in Jesus.

If we want to compare her with a figure in the New Testament, Ruth is like the Canaanite woman, poor, belonging to a despised, heathen race, who is however praised by Jesus: " 'Yes, Lord, yet even the dogs eat the crumbs that fall from their master's table.' Then Jesus answered her, 'O woman, great is your faith! Be it done for you, as you desire!' " (*Mt 15:27–28*). Jesus had also bestowed praise on his mother Mary for having faith. But it strikes us that whereas Mary had responded to the angel: "Let it be to me according to your word", here it's Jesus who has to yield to the faith of the Canaanitess: "Be it done for you, as you desire!" The Canaanitess had no connection with the Chosen People, she didn't know the history and prophecies of Israel; she simply lets herself be guided by her heart, by the feelings she experiences under Jesus's gaze. In this she reminds us of the faith and courage of Ruth.

Ruth furthermore represents *the opening of the heathen to the knowledge of the true God*. The corresponding New Testament image for this is the centurion who asks for his sick servant to be healed. "Lord, I am not worthy to have you come under my roof; but only say the word, and my servant will be healed." . . . When Jesus heard him, he marvelled, and said to those who followed him, "Truly, I say to you, not even in Israel have I found such faith. I tell you, many will come from east and west and sit at table with Abraham, Isaac, and Jacob in the kingdom of heaven, while the sons of the kingdom will be thrown into the outer darkness" (*Mt 8:8,10–12*).

The figure of Ruth proclaims *the universalism of salvation*, which was to be foretold by the prophets; Ruth introduces it into the people of God, into the Davidic line that Jesus was to bring to perfection.

Reading the *Book of Ruth* in this sense, the roots of Jesus himself may be found in it.

In connexion with this, I remind you of two other important Old Testament texts. One is the *Book of Jonah*, which breaks with the particularism in which the post-exilic community was tempted to shut itself up (as we have seen in that passage from the *Book of Nehemiah*), and instead preaches an extraordinarily open universalism.

In the story of Jonah all the characters are sympathetic, as they are in *Ruth*: the heathen sailors like Jonah very much; the king and inhabitants of Nineveh are well disposed towards him. Only Jonah is rebellious; God however has pity on him.

Jesus was to take his stand on the faith and conversion of the Ninevites to refute the scribes and Pharisees: "The

men of Nineveh will arise at the judgement with this genera-
tion and condemn it; for they repented at the preaching of
Jonah, and behold, something greater than Jonah is here"
(*Mt 12:41*).

The other text consists of a strange prediction of Isaiah's,
emphasising a very moving universalism. The Lord will
become the liberator of the oppressed Egyptian people and
actually go so far as to call them "his people": "In that
day there will be five cities in the land of Egypt which speak
the language of Canaan and swear allegiance to the Lord
of hosts. One of these will be called the City of the Sun.

In that day there will be an altar to the Lord in the midst
of the land of Egypt, and a pillar to the Lord at its border.
It will be a sign and a witness to the Lord of hosts in the
land of Egypt; when they cry to the Lord because of op-
pressors he will send them a saviour, and will defend and
deliver them. And the Lord will make himself known to
the Egyptians; and the Egyptians will know the Lord in that
day and worship with sacrifice and burnt offering, and they
will make vows to the Lord and perform them. And the
Lord will smite Egypt, smiting and healing, and they will
return to the Lord, and he will heed their supplications and
heal them.

In that day there will be a highway from Egypt to Assyria,
and the Assyrian will come into Egypt, and the Egyptian
into Assyria, and the Egyptians will worship with the
Assyrians.

In that day Israel will be the third with Egypt and Assyria,
a blessing in the midst of the earth, whom the Lord of hosts
has blessed, saying, 'Blessed be Egypt my people, and
Assyria the work of my hands, and Israel my heritage' "
(*Is 19:18–25*).

This stupendous promise of messianic blessing, of
reunion of all peoples in love of the Lord, has its roots in
the *Book of Ruth*, is glimpsed at a few peak-moments of
Israelite history, and is brought about at the end of the ages
when Jesus Christ our Lord and Universal King delivers
everything to the Father.

I invite you to reconsider the figure of Ruth also to

help you contemplate how God comes to meet us in every circumstance of our lives, but comes to meet us as the One who loves each of us and who loves all of us, who wants to bless all human beings.

Let us pray for all the communities entrusted to us, for all the peoples of the Church and for those with whom we live, that the love and blessing of the Lord may come down on all mankind.

THE GREATEST IS THE ONE WHO SERVES
(Homily for the Feast of St James the Apostle)

James known as the Great was the first of the apostles to suffer martyrdom. As one of the patrons of Christian Europe, you might think him entitled to a more honourable gospel text for his liturgical feast, such as for instance the one describing how he and his brother John were called.

Matthew 20:20–28 is a curious story, a bit out of true and slightly disturbing. It reminds us of *Mark 3* where Jesus's relatives intervene in his life, actually maintaining he is out of his wits; Jesus rebuffs their intervention because it interferes with his freedom.

Similarly in our text today there is an intervention which makes the apostles agitated and indignant.

The incident is well known: the mother of James and John asks Jesus for her sons to sit, in the Kingdom of God, one at the right hand and the other at the left hand of the Lord.

Jesus then turns directly to the two apostles and starts a dialogue. The teaching is then extended to the other ten disciples.

1) Who wanted this unpleasant encounter between the mother of the sons of Zebedee and Jesus? Was it she, or the sons?

Behind this undoubtedly historical scene, we descry a family drama.

Imagine that James and John have gone home for a few days and their mother has asked them how they are getting on. "Very well," they reply, "it's fine being with Jesus because he's a potent master, he likes us very much, shows great affection for John, may even make him his successor. He took us both up a mountain and showed us a secret we aren't allowed to tell anyone about".

Their mother is satisfied with this answer; at the same time she has a feeling they may be holding something back.

She insists on knowing, and the sons admit they would prefer it if their role were more precisely defined.

It also happens that we too say: My role isn't clear, I want to know exactly who I am in the Church.

Under their mother's questioning, the sons explain that sometimes Peter seems to come first while at other times it seems to be John.

At this point, their mother reassures them: "You just leave this to me?"

Naturally James and John raise objections, they are scared of losing face. But she won't be put off and insists they arrange for her to have a meeting — just a brief one — with the Master.

The sons give in to her and she prepares a long speech, rehearses it, alters it and finally decides: You are a great master — she will say — you are good, you love my two boys; and they love you too. . . Gradually she will make him understand that they deserve a position of honour. If he listens to me, I shall thank him; if he says no, I shall insist on knowing what they have done wrong.

People who don't obtain the position, the office, the commission they were hoping for, often get to wondering: What did I do wrong? What was my mistake? And it isn't always easy to convince them the reason why that particular job was entrusted to someone else had nothing whatever to do with them, there was no mistake on their part at all.

Anyhow, when their mother meets Jesus, she forgets the speech she has prepared. Instead, she clumsily blurts out: "These are my two boys; give orders for them to sit, one on your right and the other on your left, in your Kingdom" (cf *v. 21*).

Her intervention goes all wrong, reminding us of Martha's words at Bethany: Order my sister to help me (cf *Lk 10:40*).

The woman is so confused and worked up about her sons that she makes herself and them appear in a very poor light.

2) How does Jesus behave? We might have suggested he should give her a straight answer that it couldn't be done, that the primacy had henceforth been entrusted to Peter,

that parents had no right to interfere in the running of the ministry.

Or we might have advised him to temporise.

Instead, Jesus begins by making a severe comment, which nonetheless doesn't put the mother in the wrong: "You do not know what you are asking". These are words that inform without wounding. He has understood how much she loves her sons and treats her tactfully, trying to explain that perhaps what she is asking isn't the best thing for them.

Then he adds: "Are you able to drink the cup that I am to drink?" (*v. 22*).

The two boys' reply, "We are able", evidently doesn't please Jesus, who would have preferred to hear them say: What is the cup and what is meant by drinking it?

Notice Jesus's sagacity: he turns to the sons, not to the mother, having guessed she has expressed a wish that embarrasses them; he wants to help them.

So he goes on: "You will drink my cup". He doesn't say "willingly" because he already knows the apostles won't immediately enter his vision of faith.

There will be a time when they refuse the cup and there will be a time when they accept it. James really and truly drank the cup at his martyrdom.

Again, the level of the discourse rises: "But to sit at my right hand and at my left is not mine to grant, but it is for those for whom it has been prepared by my Father" (*v. 23*). By his own example, Jesus points out that position has no importance: I myself am not concerned about it. I let the Father do as he wishes, since all that matters is his will.

3) At this point begins the magnificent exhortation which I shall leave for you to meditate on: the greatest is the one who serves. A mother's ill-judged intervention becomes the occasion for an extraordinary piece of teaching on Jesus's part; it constitutes the very law of the Church and ends in a Christological confession: "The Son of man came not to be served but to serve, and to give his life as a ransom for many" (*v. 28*).

We cannot read these words without blushing,

especially I, since service is the motto of bishops, service to the point of giving up one's life.

4)   The passage in the *Second Letter to the Corinthians*, which has been read out today, is a good commentary on the gospel text: "We have this treasure in earthen vessels, to show that the transcendent power belongs to God and not to us . . . ." (cf *2 Cor 4:7–15*).

James, John and their mother are poor, short-sighted people who haven't intuitively grasped the grandeur of the Kingdom of God. Earthen vessels therefore and things of no worth. They do however contain an incredible treasure: John, the gospel of contemplation of the Word; James, the strength of martyrdom. Precisely because of this, they undergo every kind of trial without being crushed, they are persecuted but not forsaken, perplexed but not driven to despair (cf *v. 8*).

Paul uses the terms of material poverty to characterise the apostolic life, and an apostle shouldn't be ashamed of this, since this sort of poverty contains God's treasure.

We are all a bit like James and John, concerned about our role, about getting a prestigious post. What really counts however are the marvels the Lord works in us. I have seen them during these days of Exercises, as I have got to know you individually, hearing your life-stories, knowing the examples you set in courage and abnegation, in prayer and self-giving, sometimes at risk of your lives. I have admired them in you and in your people, in this Church, in all whom I have met; they are the evidence of the power of the Risen Christ. The Church of God is led by the Holy Spirit, even in the humblest beginnings of the young Churches, and we cannot but give praise and thanks.

As I look at you, I think particularly of Europe and its task of being a factor in uniting the world.

The day will come, according to Isaiah's prophecy, when Egypt, that is to say Africa, Assur, that is to say Asia, and Israel will be one, with Israel at the centre.

Peter and James came from Jerusalem to bring Christianity to Europe. But the way is long, still very long. We are called to pray and work, always contemplating the ideal of unity; the celebration of the Eucharist is the first great work of the Church, since by this we can unite the world in symbol and in fact.

That is the grace we ask for at this Mass, uniting us for the last time round the Blessed Sacrament, true centre of the Church and universe.